knitgrrl 2

Learn to Knit with 16 All-New Patterns

PHOTOGRAPHY BY
SHANNON FAGAN,
CHRISTINE OKEY,
AND TAMAS JAKAB
ILLUSTRATIONS
BY KATHLEEN
JACQUES

Shannon Okey

SENIOR ACQUISITIONS EDITOR: Julie Mazur
EDITOR: Linda Hetzer
DESIGNER: Margo Mooney
SENIOR PRODUCTION MANAGER: Ellen Greene

First published in 2006 by Watson-Guptill Publications,
Nielsen Business Media, a division of The Nielsen Company
770 Broadway, New York, NY 10003
www.watsonguptill.com

Library of Congress Control Number: 2005934176

ISBN: 0-8230-2619-1

Printed in China

First printing, 2006

3 4 5 6 7 8 9 / 14 13 12 11 10 09 08 07

For Tamas, as ever

ACKNOWLEDGMENTS

In the acknowledgments to the first KnitGrrl book I thanked the usual suspects: designers, yarn companies, photographers, models, knitting colleagues, and my technical editor. They've all been a vital part of this second book, too. However, I'd like to offer special thanks to my editors, Julie Mazur and Linda Hetzer, to the book designer, Margo Mooney, to all my readers (both online and off!), and to my mom. Of course, Tamas, Anezka, and Spike took care of me while I wrote this book—I wouldn't be able to do it without them!

contents

introduction

JOIN the KNITTING REVOLUTION!

K nitting is an ever-enjoyable learning process. From my very first "a-ha!" moment figuring out something tricky with the needles to today, I'm always picking up something new. If I get bored with one style or type of knitting (hat burnout! cabling exhaustion!), I can switch to something else for a while…and I don't have to buy all new equipment.

There's always something different to try, too. With each new type of yarn on the market, my knitting possibilities increase exponentially. Yarn shapes knitting design as much (and sometimes more!) than the human designer behind the needles. Need proof? Try substituting the absolute opposite of the recommended

web

Check out **www.knitgrrl.com** to ask questions, post photos of your projects, chat with other knitters, and get lots of new ideas!

O, let me teach you how to knit again!

–William Shakespeare, *Titus Andronicus*, Act V, Scene III

yarn in a pattern sometime. The results may be exciting, or an outright failure; but either way, trying different things helps you grow as a knitter.

All of the basic techniques you'll need are included here, just as they were in the first KnitGrrl book—from putting the yarn on your needles to taking it off again, and everything in between! We've added a few new techniques, too—they'll not only help you with specific patterns but also expand your overall knitting skills.

One special note about the yarn used in these projects. Sometimes a yarn company discontinues a type of yarn and you can't buy it anymore (this happens more than you'd think!). If you're having a hard time finding the yarn for a project, it doesn't mean you can't knit that pattern. It just means you have the opportunity to pick another yarn you think will work. Ask your local yarn store for advice, talk to other friends who knit…. Chances are someone else has found a good substitute yarn, or maybe even a completely unexpected one that works perfectly! You have the power to change, to knit, and to create something fabulous. I can't wait to see what you come up with—visit knitgrrl.com and show off your creations!

knitting for charity

Looking for a worthwhile project to do with your friends, a club, or your classmates? Consider knitting for charity! Yarn stores often sponsor a "mitten tree" during the holiday season for knitters to decorate with handmade mittens, scarves, and hats. When the tree is full, the items are donated to people who need them. Why not work with more experienced knitters to help make items for your local mitten tree? Chances are you'll pick up plenty of knitting tips from them, too. To make it even more fun, you can suggest that the store host a contest for the most creative item.

If your yarn store doesn't have a mitten tree, ask if you can start one! Or look for a local charity that accepts hand-knit items. See page 94 for a website that lists such charities across the country.

what a girl needs

In any craft, it helps to know about the tools you'll be using before you begin. Become familiar with yarn and needles, plus all the other little things that knitters use.... Everything will make much more sense that way!

YARN

When it comes to knitting, yarn is numero uno—the most important thing. Most patterns will tell you exactly what kind of yarn to use, so the only thing you need to choose is the color. But if you're feeling adventurous, you can decide to use one of a zillion different kinds of yarn. Choosing the right yarn for a project isn't as tough as it sounds—it can actually be fun. Want to make a scarf that's soft and fluffy? Eyelash yarn might be right for the job. What about a bag strong enough for your beach gear? Think about cotton. Are you making a funky collar for your jean jacket? Then how about yarn that looks fuzzy or furry?

Looking at the shelves and shelves of yarn in your local store can make your head spin. But believe it or not, the thousands of yarn types can be grouped into a few simple categories, such as fiber, texture, and weight. (And of course, color, but more on that on page 12.) Once you "get" these different categories, yarn will make much more sense. Here's the scoop on each.

FIBER Every yarn is made up of fibers—the fibers can be natural, synthetic, or a mix of both. Natural yarns are made of animal fibers such as wool, silk, angora, alpaca, mohair, and cashmere, and/or plant fibers such as cotton, linen, and rayon. Synthetic yarns are made of acrylic, nylon, polyester, and many other man-made materials.

TEXTURE The texture of a yarn refers to how smooth it is. If you're a new knitter, you may want to start with a very smooth-textured yarn such as worsted wool or cotton—these make it easy to see your stitches. But you can also try yarns that are thick-and-thin, solid or tweed, flat, bumpy, or twisted.

Yarns come in so many sizes, weights, textures, fibers, and colors—the sky's the limit!

WEIGHT Yarn is also classified by thickness, or weight. The thinnest, or lightest, yarn is called super fine, while the thickest, or heaviest, yarn is super bulky. Different patterns call for yarns of different weights. For example, a thick winter scarf would probably call for a heavier-weight yarn, while a summer tank top would use a lighter yarn.

The Craft Yarn Council of America has developed a chart to classify yarn by weight, giving each weight a special symbol. Here's our version of the chart below.

NOVELTY YARN Knitters call any kind of fluffy, furry, shiny, unusual yarn novelty yarn—in short, any yarn that has a special effect or unique look when knitted. Fake fur, eyelash yarn, railroad ribbon, and thick-and-thin textured yarn are just a few kinds. Novelty yarns are great for adding funky touches to any knitting project.

Here are just a few of the cool novelty yarns available. Shown clockwise from left: pink fake fur, "paper" tape with nylon squiggles, thick-and-thin, faux angora, and railroad ribbon yarns.

This chart shows you how yarn is put into categories by weight. If you like a pattern but want to switch the yarn, you can usually pick another one in the same weight category. You'll learn more about substituting yarn on page 30.

THE CRAFT YARN COUNCIL OF AMERICA'S STANDARD YARN WEIGHT SYSTEM

YARN WEIGHT CATEGORY	SYMBOL	TYPES OF YARN	HOW MANY STITCHES MAKE 4 INCHES OF KNITTED FABRIC?	RECOMMENDED NEEDLE SIZES (US)	RECOMMENDED NEEDLE SIZES (METRIC)
Super fine	1 SUPER FINE	Sock, fingering, baby	27–32 sts	1–3	2.25–3.25 mm
Fine	2 FINE	Sport, baby	23–26 sts	3–5	3.25–3.75 mm
Light	3 LIGHT	DK, light worsted	21–24 sts	5–7	3.75–4.5 mm
Medium	4 MEDIUM	Worsted, afghan, aran	16–20 sts	7–9	4.5–5.5 mm
Bulky	5 BULKY	Chunky, craft, rug	12–15 sts	9–11	5.5–8 mm
Super bulky	6 SUPER BULKY	Bulky, roving	6–11 sts	11 and larger	8 mm and larger

reading a yarn label

Most yarn comes wrapped in a label with lots of important information on it, from the manufacturer's name to instructions on caring for your knit item. Here is a breakdown of what's what.

FIBER CONTENT This is what the yarn is made of, such as wool or cotton. If the yarn is a blend, it will give you the percentage of each fiber.

DYE LOT NUMBER When yarn is dyed, it is given a dye lot number. If you are making a large item that calls for several skeins of yarn, be sure to buy skeins with the same dye lot number. This means they were dyed together in the same batch and will be exactly the same color. Even white yarn has a dye lot number!

WEIGHT AND LENGTH The weight will be given in ounces or grams. The length will be given in yards or meters (often both!).

GAUGE The gauge is the number of stitches and rows in a 4-inch square, using the recommended size needles. (More about gauge on page 30.)

CARE INSTRUCTIONS This is what the manufacturer suggests when washing and drying your knit item. Many (but not all) labels use symbols like these. The ones shown here mean, from left to right: hand wash, do not iron, and dry flat. If in doubt, you can almost never go wrong with careful hand-washing! (See page 93.) For projects that use more than one kind of yarn, follow the directions for the most delicate yarn used.

tip If you can't find enough skeins of the same dye lot number and need to buy two different ones, alternate yarn from the two dye lots every few rows and the color variation will be less obvious.

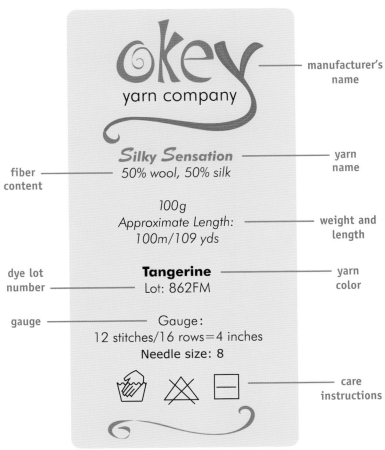

okey yarn company — manufacturer's name

Silky Sensation — yarn name
50% wool, 50% silk — fiber content

100g
Approximate Length:
100m/109 yds — weight and length

Tangerine — yarn color
Lot: 862FM — dye lot number

Gauge: — gauge
12 stitches/16 rows=4 inches
Needle size: 8

— care instructions

choosing colors

Studies have shown that most knitters just choose the same color yarn shown in the pattern photo. If you love the color in the photo and want your project to look exactly the same, go for it! But why not take a leap and express yourself by choosing a different color? That's the great thing about knitting—you can make something that is truly unique! Take the time to choose a color (or combo of colors) you love. If you have a difficult time choosing, take a look at this color wheel—what jumps out at you first? You might be surprised! We're often attracted to colors we don't think we "like," and first impressions of color are very powerful.

Experiment with your favorite colors to see which combinations you prefer. Put together items you already have in order to see how the colors look, and then buy corresponding yarns. Do you always wear your rose-colored shirt with khaki pants? Try rose and khaki together in a scarf. Do you like the way your green purse looks on top of your purple sheets? Knit a tank top that combines the two. You're the designer, and you're in control.

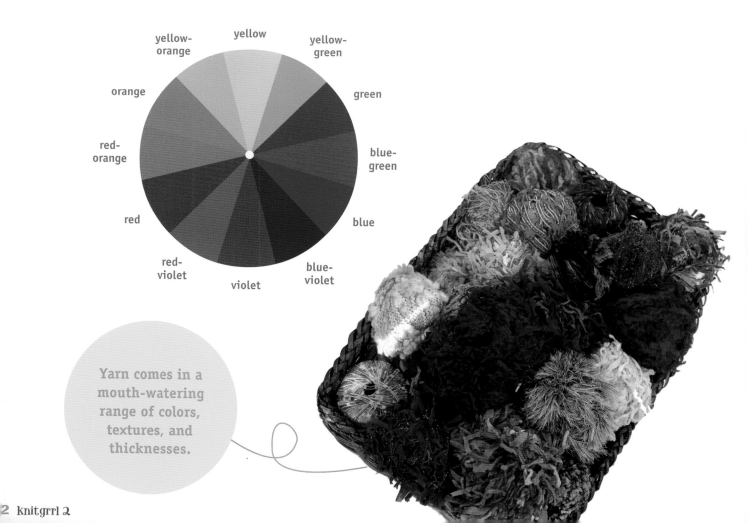

yellow-orange · yellow · yellow-green · orange · green · red-orange · blue-green · red · blue · red-violet · blue-violet · violet

Yarn comes in a mouth-watering range of colors, textures, and thicknesses.

What's Your Color?

So many colors, so little time…. If you don't already have a favorite palette of colors, take this quiz and find out which ones might be right for you!

1 IF YOU PICKED A NEW IM SCREEN NAME, WHAT WOULD IT BE?

A gottaBme
B hooked_on_harry
C sweetie_pie
D soccergirl
E n2art

2 YOUR IDEA OF FUN IS:

A Dancing all night at a party.
B Getting lost in an amazing new book.
C Going shopping with your best friend.
D Playing in a championship soccer game.
E Doing artwork for your website.

3 WHAT'S YOUR FAVORITE CLASS?

A Drama.
B English.
C Home Ec.
D Gym.
E Art.

4 HOW DO YOU DO YOUR HAIR?

A Depends—what's the latest style?
B Straight and long, but nothing fancy.
C You like to use pretty barrettes and ponytail holders.
D Short and easy to care for. Who has time for it?
E You're always experimenting with braids and new looks—sometimes it's even purple!

5 YOUR DREAM VACATION IS:

A A week in LA touring movie studios and celeb-watching. Maybe you'll even get spotted by an agent!
B A week at the beach with nothing to do but relax, read, and hang out.
C A week at a spa, with all the manicures and facials you want!
D Skiing in the mountains with a bunch of friends.
E A trip to Paris. All those museums and cafés to explore!

6 YOU ARE LOOKING FOR A NEW VOLUNTEER ACTIVITY. WHICH WOULD IT BE?

A Putting on a play to raise money for local charities.
B Teaching adults how to read.
C Playing games with kids in the hospital.
D Building houses for those in need.
E Painting a mural in your local community center.

7 YOU NOTICE YOUR CRUSH WALKING TOWARD YOU IN SCHOOL. WHAT DO YOU DO?

A "Accidentally" drop your books so he has to help you pick them up.
B Turn away quickly—you hope he didn't catch you looking at him!
C Flash your sweetest smile and ask him for help carrying your stuff.
D Wave and say, "Hey, did ya catch the game last night?"
E Give him a flyer for your band's next gig.

8 YOUR BEST FRIEND WOULD DESCRIBE YOU AS:

A Fun-loving and dramatic.
B Super smart and a good listener.
C A social butterfly with lots of friends.
D Athletic and always on the go.
E Creative and artsy.

Scoring

MOSTLY As – You love attention! Make a statement with bold colors such as reds, oranges, and metallics.

MOSTLY Bs – You have a sweet, calming disposition that will be happiest in sunny yellows, greens, and blues.

MOSTLY Cs – Pink is a girl's best friend! Bring out your feminine nature with pastels such as pinks, light blues, and peaches.

MOSTLY Ds – Fun-loving and outdoorsy, you will be most comfortable in natural colors such as earthy browns, grays, and greens.

MOSTLY Es – Your artsy soul will be inspired by deep jewel tones such as magenta, purple, and indigo blue.

NEEDLES and OTHER TOOLS

After yarn, the second most important item you will use to knit is knitting needles. There are many kinds to choose from, some more common than others. Most needles are made from plastic, wood, bamboo, or metal.

Straight needles are what most people think of as "knitting needles"—long, smooth needles that are pointy on one end, with a knob on the other.

Circular needles are two needles connected by a flexible plastic cord. Circulars have a lot of advantages over straight needles. They keep the project's entire weight evenly balanced in the center, which keeps your wrists from supporting all that yarn. (You'd be surprised how heavy it can get!) Your hands, wrists, and elbows are held in a more natural position, and some knitters swear that they can knit faster with circular needles. Circular needles can be used for almost any pattern, even if it is designed for straights. Here's how: every time you reach the end of a row, turn your knitting around, and start going across the row again, just as you would with straight needles. Try both circular and straight needles and see which you like better.

Double-pointed needles, or **DPNs,** are straight and pointy at both ends. DPNs can be used to knit small tubes or finish off tight circles. They're also great for making i-cord (see page 90).

Needles come in various sizes, and patterns and needle packages will usually list both U.S. and metric sizes (see conversion chart, above). So which size needles should you buy? One option is to buy whatever size needles you need, when you need them. If you're knitting a hat that requires size 10s, buy 10s. Next week, if you need 5s for something else...buy those, too. The only problem with this is that it becomes very expensive very quickly. And, of course, you might find yourself stuck without the needles you need just when the stores have closed for the weekend.

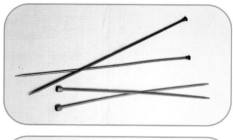

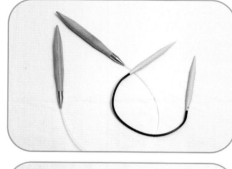

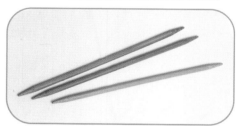

NEEDLE SIZES (US)	NEEDLE SIZES (METRIC)
3	3.25 mm
4	3.5 mm
5	3.75 mm
6	4 mm
7	4.5 mm
8	5 mm
9	5.5 mm
10	6 mm
10.5	6.5 mm
11	8 mm
13	9 mm
15	10 mm
17	12.75 mm
19	15 mm
35	19 mm
50	25 mm

A second option is the Denise needle system, shown below. This is a kit that you can use to make any number of different size circular needles. You just pick out a pair of needle tips in whatever size you need and twist them onto the end of a flexible cord. If you need to switch needle size, just twist off the needle tips and twist on another size.

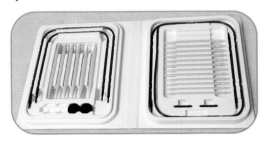

OTHER TOOLS

Here's a list of other knitting tools you'll need. They can be found at most craft stores and at all good yarn stores.

Tapestry needles (sometimes called **yarn needles**) are a must-have. They look like big sewing needles with an eye large enough to thread yarn through, and have blunt tips. Tapestry needles are used to weave in loose ends after you've changed balls of yarn and/or after you've finished a project. You will need a tapestry needle for every pattern in this book, and probably every pattern you'll ever knit! They are the fastest and easiest way to weave in ends when you're finished knitting.

You'll need a small pair of **scissors** to cut yarn. You probably already have scissors, but it helps to have a small pair you can carry with you in your knitting bag. Some even fold up!

Stitch markers help you keep track of where you are in your pattern. They sit on your needle between two stitches like a little reminder, so you know that you have to do something when you get to that particular stitch. Some stitch markers are simple plastic rings; others are fancy.

A **row counter** (sometimes called a *kacha-kacha*, for the sound it makes) is used to keep track of how many rows you've knitted. Every time you come to the end of a row, you twist the side or click the button and the number goes up by one.

Crochet hooks aren't just used in crochet. They're good to have when you drop a stitch or need to pull yarn through something that's too small for your fingers.

Stitch holders look like huge safety pins. If you need to hold some stitches in reserve, you can slip them onto the holder and keep them separate while you continue knitting elsewhere. They come in handy, but are not necessary. If you just need to hold a few stitches temporarily, you can slip them onto an extra circular needle or even a DPN.

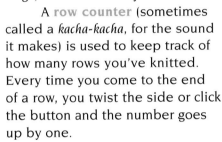

READING PATTERNS

Before you begin to knit any pattern, it's important to read through the pattern thoroughly to make sure you have all the materials and understand how the finished item will be put together.

In this book, each pattern gives the name of the designer, the skills you need to complete the pattern, the finished measurements and/or size, the materials needed (both yarn and tools), the pattern gauge (more on that later), the pattern itself, and any special directions for finishing up.

If a pattern uses more than one color of yarn, they are indicated as Color 1, Color 2, and so on.

A pair of asterisks (* *) means that whatever directions are between them should be repeated. For example, "*Knit 3, purl 1* to end of row" means that you should knit 3 stitches and then purl 1, over and over, until you reach the end of the row.

We've written our pattern directions almost entirely in plain English, but most patterns you'll see elsewhere are written with special abbreviations (such as k for knit). Check out the abbreviations chart opposite for a list of the most common ones, and keep it handy for when you start using patterns from magazines or websites.

There *are* a few abbreviations we do use in this book, because the directions were too wordy to write out every time. These are k2tog (knit 2 together), k2tog tbl (knit 2 together through back loop), SSK (slip, slip, knit), and SKP (slip, knit, pass slipped stitch over). Besides, getting used to these abbreviations will make it even easier when you start using other patterns!

getting warmed up

Each chapter in this book introduces new skills, and the projects generally get harder toward the end of the book. But this doesn't mean you have to do the projects in order! When you want to start a project, check out the skills listed at the beginning. If there's something you haven't learned yet, flip to the page that teaches that skill, read through the directions, look at the step-by-step photos, and even practice with a spare piece of yarn. That way, you'll feel confident when you actually start working on your project. If this is your first time knitting, you might want to begin with the first project in the book, the Ooh-la-la Flip-Flops on page 33. You can make them quickly and without having to worry too much about the fit.

Knitting Abbreviations

Knitting abbreviations may look like secret code, but they're really very simple. Here is a list of the most common ones. Keep this page handy and use it as reference when you start working on other patterns.

* *	repeat directions between * * as many times as indicated
alt	alternate
approx	approximately
beg	begin[ning]
BO	bind off (cast off)
cab	cable
CC	contrasting color
cn	cable needle
CO	cast on
cont	continue[ing]
dec	decrease[ing]
DPN	double-pointed needles[s]
foll	follow[s][ing]
g	grams
inc	increase[ing]
incl	including
inst	instructions
k	knit
k1fb	knit in the front and back of the next stitch (increase)
k tbl	knit through back of loop
k2tog	knit 2 stitches together (decrease)
m	meter[s]
MC	main color
m1	make 1 stitch (increase)
mm	millimeters
mult	multiple
opp	opposite

oz	ounce[s]
p	purl
p2tog	purl 2 together (decrease)
patt[s]	pattern[s]
psso	pass slipped stitch[es] over
rem	remaining
rep	repeat
rev St st	reverse stockinette stitch
RS	right side[s]
rnd[s]	round[s]
sc	single crochet
SKP	slip 1 stitch, knit 1 stitch, pass the slipped stitch over the knitted stitch (decrease)
SSK	slip 2 stitches as if to knit, knit 2 stitches together (decrease)
SSP	slip 2 stitches as if to purl, purl 2 together (decrease)
sl	slip
slp	slip 1 stitch as if to purl
sl st	slip stitch
st[s]	stitch[es]
St st	stockinette stitch
tbl	through back of loop[s]
tog	together
WS	wrong side[s]
YO	yarn over
YO2	a yarn over with the yarn wrapped twice around the needle

knitting 101

Ready to start knitting? Grab a pair of needles (any size) and some scrap yarn, and practice these basic stitches before starting your first project. If you're already a pro, use this chapter as a refresher class in case you've gotten rusty!

WHAT is KNITTING?

Knitting is simply looping yarn around a pair of sticks, called knitting needles. All knitting is made up of only two stitches—really! There's the knit stitch and the purl stitch, which is just a knit stitch done backwards and inside out (not nearly as complicated as it sounds).

To begin, you make loops on one needle. This is called **casting on.** Then you use a second needle to knit or purl each loop, or **stitch.** You continue knitting or purling every stitch on your needle, one after the other (if you're following a pattern, it will tell you what to do). As you go, the stitches will transfer from one needle to the other. When you've knit or purled all the stitches on the needle, you've finished one **row.** Then you just swap the needles so the one holding the stitches is back in your nondominant hand (for me, the left) and continue on the next row. If you're knitting a **round** on circular needles, you won't need to switch hands, you'll just pass the stitch marker and keep going (more on that later).

it takes two!

You may think that knit stitches and purl stitches look pretty much the same, but take a closer look. The two stitches actually make very different shapes on the needle. It's important to be able to tell the difference between the two when you're knitting.

KNIT STITCH

A knit stitch forms a V, and rows of knit stitches form a series of Vs.

PURL STITCH

A purl stitch creates a short, horizontal bump. Rows of purl stitches look like horizontal lines.

CASTING ON

Putting the first row of knitting on your needle is called **casting on**. There are many ways to cast on—here we'll show you the most common one, the long-tail cast-on.

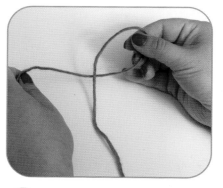 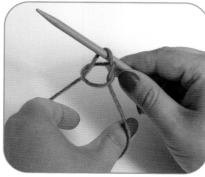 

1 Start by making a slipknot and tighten it slightly around the needle.

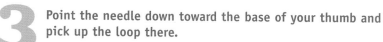

 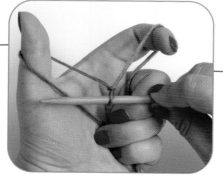 

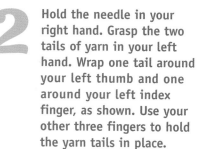

2 Hold the needle in your right hand. Grasp the two tails of yarn in your left hand. Wrap one tail around your left thumb and one around your left index finger, as shown. Use your other three fingers to hold the yarn tails in place.

3 Point the needle down toward the base of your thumb and pick up the loop there.

4 Bring the loop up and around, then place the needle tip over and through the loop that's running around your index finger.

5 Bring the right loop through the thumb loop.

tip If you find you are casting on too tightly, use the next higher needle size. Then, once you've finished casting on your first row, slip the stitches back onto the correct size needle.

6 Release your thumb and index finger and pull down on the tails to tighten the first loop onto the needle.

7 Repeat steps 2–6 to cast on more stitches. Your pattern will tell you how many. Your needle will move in a sort of sideways figure-8 as it rotates through the loops.

tip Stop and count the stitches on your needle every once in a while to make sure you are casting on the right number.

8 When you are ready to start your first stitch, you will put the right-hand needle into the first loop on the left-hand needle.

HOW to KNIT

Now that you have your first row cast onto the needle, you're ready to start knitting. As we said earlier, all knitting is made up of just two stitches—the knit stitch and the purl stitch. Let's take a close look at how each stitch is made.

The Knit Stitch

1 Put the needle through the stitch from front to back. (These photos show a row already in progress. If you were starting a row, you would start with the first stitch on your needle.)

2 Wrap the yarn around the tip of the needle you pushed through from back to front.

3 Pull the needle with the new yarn wrapped around it through to the front.

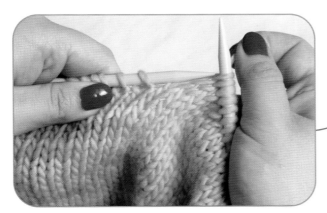

4 Slide the needle with the new stitch off to the right. You just knit a stitch!

tip Some patterns will refer to your "working yarn." This is the long strand of yarn that extends from the ball or skein you are using to your needle.

holding your needles and yarn

In this book, all of the photos show the "English," or "American," style of knitting. In this style, you hold the needles close to their tips and use your dominant hand (the one you write with) to wrap the yarn around the needle. (Some people prefer the "Continental" style, where you wrap the yarn with your non-dominant hand.) As you begin to knit, remember that it takes time to get used to balancing needles and yarn. Don't grip the needles too tightly or your hands will get tired almost immediately!

The Purl Stitch

1 Put the needle through the stitch from back to front.

2 Wrap the yarn around the needle you pushed through from front to back.

3 Push the needle with the new yarn wrapped around it through to the back.

4 Slide the needle with the new stitch off to the right. You've just purled a stitch.

CREATING KNIT FABRIC

When you combine knit and purl stitches in certain ways, you create different kinds of knit fabric. The three most basic types are called garter (sometimes called "garter stitch"), stockinette, and reverse stockinette. The photos below show what each of these looks like.

When you knit "flat" on straight needles, your knitted work has a front, sometimes called the public side or right side, and a back, or wrong side (often abbreviated RS and WS). Every time you finish a row and switch your needles, you are switching from the front to the back, or vice versa. When you knit a tube on circular needles or DPNs, the wrong side is automatically on the inside and you don't have to worry about switching hands.

garter stitch

To make the garter stitch, all you do is knit every single stitch, in every row. Two rows of knitting create what's called a ridge. Some patterns written for garter stitch will ask you to count ridges instead of rows, because they're easier to keep track of.

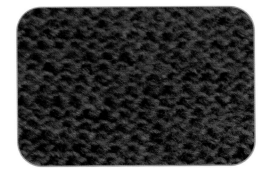

stockinette

If you knit each row on the right side of your work (the front) and purl each row on the wrong side (the back), you get what's called the stockinette stitch. Stockinette is probably what you think of when you hear "knitting"— a fabric made up of little Vs lined up in rows.

reverse stockinette

If you flip the work over and look at the stockinette stitch from the back (or wrong side, where all the little purl bumps live), the pattern looks different. This is called reverse stockinette. Some yarns look more interesting on the bumpy purl side than they do on the right side, and the pattern will intentionally place the purl side on public view. You don't have to do anything differently to make reverse stockinette, but if it's meant to be shown, you'll weave in ends on the other side of the fabric when you're done.

JOINING NEW YARN

Most patterns use more than one ball of yarn, and some have you alternate two colors of yarn at one time (like the Striped Pencil Purse on page 48). So what do you do when the first ball runs out or you want to change colors? Easy—just join a new ball. Here's how. In these photos, the blue yarn is "new."

1 Leave a tail 3–4 inches long hanging from the old yarn. Take the new yarn and fold over the first 4 inches. Insert the needle into the next stitch as usual. Loop the new yarn over the needle.

2 Pull the needle through, just as you would for a normal stitch.

3 Complete the stitch with the new yarn by sliding it off the needle. Now just continue knitting using the new yarn.

4 For the first few stitches with the new yarn, you may need to hold onto both old and new yarn ends to keep your stitches from getting too sloppy. If they do get a little loose, just give the two yarn ends a tug.

BINDING OFF

Okay, so you've finally finished your project—congratulations!—and it's time to get the knitting off of your needles. This is called binding off.

1 Knit the first two stitches of your last row. Make your stitches very loose and sloppy. (Trust me—the tighter they are, the tougher it will be.) If you are using circular needles, as in these photos, start at the beginning of the last round.

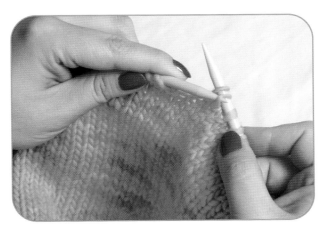 

2 Using the tip of your left-hand needle, lift the first stitch (the one on the right) over the second stitch. Think of it as leapfrogging over the second stitch.

4 Knit another stitch, then repeat steps 2–3 with those two stitches. Keep repeating these steps until there is only one stitch left on the left-hand needle. Cut your yarn, leaving a tail 6–8 inches long. Insert the tail through the last stitch and pull to tighten.

3 Drop the stitch off in the middle.

WEAVING in ENDS

When a project is done, you'll end up with "tails" of yarn hanging off your project. The way to get rid of them is to weave them into the wrong side of the knit fabric. This is called weaving in ends.

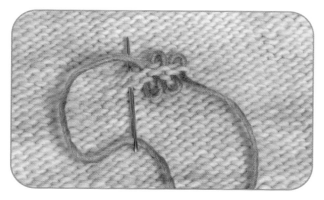

Tails always come in pairs, and you need to weave each tail in separately. Weave the yarn end on the right into stitches to the left, and vice versa. This prevents a hole from appearing on the right side of the project.

Thread one of the tails onto a tapestry needle (here, the blue yarn is the tail). Carefully weave it through 1–2 inches on the wrong side. In this photo, the yarn end is woven through purl bumps, with extra sticking out so you can see where they're going. (In real life, you would pull the yarn firmly and the yarn ends would disappear behind the bumps.) When you're done, do the same with the other tail.

SEAMING

Sometimes you'll knit a project in pieces that then have to be sewn together. Seaming, or grafting, is a way to join two pieces of knit fabric together. It's as easy as weaving in ends.

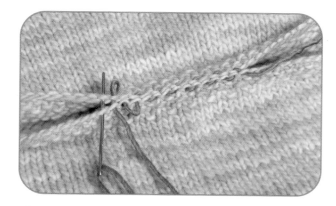

Place the two knitted pieces next to each other on a flat surface. Thread a tapestry needle with yarn and weave it back and forth between knitted stitches on either side. (I used blue yarn here to make it easy to see, but normally you would use the same yarn you used for the project to make it invisible.)

TWO common GOOFS

The two most common mistakes—and believe me, everyone makes them!—are accidentally dropping stitches, and adding extra ones. Luckily, these mistakes are not disastrous, and they're easy to fix.

TOO FEW STITCHES ON YOUR NEEDLE

Sometimes a stitch falls off of your needle while you're knitting. This is called dropping a stitch. If you drop a stitch and realize it right away, it's easy to put the end of the needle back into the stitch—just be careful not to twist it in the wrong direction when you put it on. But what if you dropped a stitch several rows ago? That's almost as easy to fix, but you'll need a crochet hook or tapestry needle. The photos below show you what to do.

TOO MANY STITCHES ON YOUR NEEDLE

Sometimes you might accidentally add a stitch by doing something called a yarn over, or YO. A yarn over gets added when you wrap your yarn around the needle more than once when knitting a stitch—you might do this by accident when you are first learning. (A yarn over can also be done on purpose—it creates a decorative hole, or "eyelet," and is also a way to add a stitch.) If you realize you've accidentally done this, there are two ways to fix it. Either drop the stitch on the next row by sliding it off your needle, or (if you're still on the same row) "backspace"! Slip completed stitches from your right-hand needle back onto the left until you reach the yarn over, then slide it off the end of the needle.

fixing a dropped stitch

tip It's a good idea to count stitches every once in a while as you work through a pattern to keep track of how many you have.

Find the dropped stitch. Look for a skip in the row of regular stitches that looks like a ladder rung.

Insert your crochet hook into the front of the dropped stitch loop, and put the hook around the next "rung" of the ladder. Pull the rung forward through the stitch loop. In this photo, the blue yarn is acting as the dropped stitch so you can clearly see how the hook is used to pull stitches through.

Keep pulling "rungs" through the stitch, moving up the "ladder," until you can finally put the stitch back on the knitting needle. Depending on how tightly you knit, it may be difficult to pick up the stitch the farther it's dropped, but have patience.

LONG LIVE the SWATCH!

As I write this, I am looking at a table full of swatches...dozens of them! I'm testing yarn for projects, and knitting different swatches for each combination. It's a lot of work, but it's worth it because I know how each yarn will look if I decide to use it.

So, what on earth am I talking about? A swatch is a sample piece of knitting made before you start your actual project, made with the same needles, stitches, and yarn. It's used to measure your gauge, which is the number of stitches per inch of knitting. Swatching is an important first step to make sure your gauge matches the one listed in the pattern. Imagine how frustrating it would be to spend weeks, or even months, knitting something that was the wrong size when finished! Swatching tells you if you're using the right size needles. It also comes in handy when you want to use a different yarn than what's listed in the pattern.

To knit a swatch, use the same size needles listed in the pattern and the yarn you plan to knit with. Cast on 20 stitches. If the pattern uses more than one type of stitch, choose the most common stitch for your swatch. For example, if you're knitting a scarf with a garter stitch edge but stockinette body, knit the swatch in stockinette.

Knit back and forth until your swatch is a square, at least 4 inches long by 4 inches wide—any smaller and you won't be able to measure the gauge properly. If you're using a very thick yarn, less than 20 stitches may be enough. Bind off the stitches and place the swatch on a flat surface. Be careful not to stretch it and distort your measurements.

like a different yarn better?

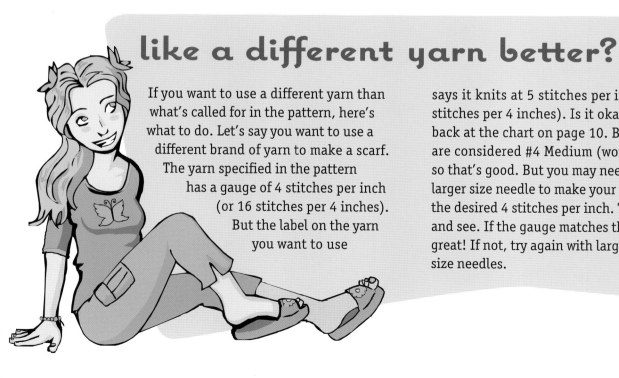

If you want to use a different yarn than what's called for in the pattern, here's what to do. Let's say you want to use a different brand of yarn to make a scarf. The yarn specified in the pattern has a gauge of 4 stitches per inch (or 16 stitches per 4 inches). But the label on the yarn you want to use says it knits at 5 stitches per inch (or 20 stitches per 4 inches). Is it okay? Look back at the chart on page 10. Both yarns are considered #4 Medium (worsted) yarns, so that's good. But you may need to use a larger size needle to make your yarn knit at the desired 4 stitches per inch. Try a swatch and see. If the gauge matches the pattern, great! If not, try again with larger or smaller size needles.

These swatches are all 20 stitches wide by 25 rows long—but look how different the sizes are! The one on the far left was knitted with size 5 needles, the one in the middle with size 8 needles, and the one on the right with size 11 needles.

Lay a ruler across the swatch and count the number of stitches from side to side in 1 inch of knitting. Do this in a couple of places to double check. Does it match your pattern's gauge? If the pattern gauge is 2.5 stitches per inch, and you have 3 stitches per inch, your finished project will be too small. Change to the next larger size needles and try your swatch again. If you have only 2 stitches per inch, it will be too large. Change to the next smaller needle size and make your swatch again. (You can unravel the one you made and reuse the yarn.) When your swatch has the same gauge as your pattern, you're good to go! (Note: Some patterns will write the gauge per 4 inches of knitting. To find out what the gauge is for 1 inch, just divide the number they give you by 4.)

A slight variation is okay for most projects; it will usually even out over the long run. More than one stitch in either direction is definitely too much. For items that are fitted, such as a hat or sweater, make sure your gauge isn't off by more than half a stitch. For something less exact, such as a belt, it's okay to be off by a little more, but keep in mind that your finished object may not look exactly like the photo.

tip In my opinion, Denise needles (see page 15) are the best needles for swatching. If you've knit a swatch and discover your gauge is not correct, switch the needle tips for the next size up or down, and just keep knitting until you find the right one!

web Got a question? Need some answers? Visit www.knitgrrl.com for help!

easy does it

Knitters, start your engines! This chapter includes three simple patterns to get you started. They're made with exciting yarns and are full of color and texture.

Ooh-la-la Flip-Flops

PATTERN BY SHANNON OKEY

skills casting on, knit stitch, binding off, seaming, weaving in ends

Strut down the beach like the movie star you are with these fluffy, oh-so-glam flip-flops! Each pair uses less than one ball of yarn, so why not make some for a friend while you're at it?

size
One size—yours!

finished measurements
Approximately 1½ x 8 inches—but measure your flip-flops to see what length and width you need.

materials
* 1 pair flip-flops
* 1 skein of Crystal Palace Splash [100% polyester; 94 yds per 100g ball] (Color used here: Carnival)
* 1 pair size 8 (5mm) needles
* Ruler
* Tapestry needle

gauge
20 stitches/28 rows = 4 inches in stockinette stitch (Note: Gauge is not critical for this project.)

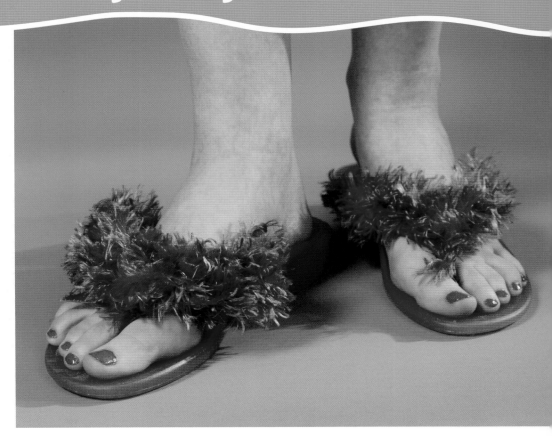

pattern
The knitted band is one long piece that covers the entire strap. Make 2, one for each flip-flop.
* Cast on 10 stitches.
* Knit in garter stitch (knit every row) for 8 inches (or as long as your flip-flop strap measures).
* Bind off, leaving a 15-inch tail.

finishing
Fold a knitted panel in half lengthwise, wrapping it around the flip-flop strap. Using a tapestry needle and the long yarn tail, sew the knitted panel over the flip-flop strap, sewing along the long side like a sleeve. Weave in any loose ends. Repeat for the other flip-flop.

Beach-Read Book Covers

PATTERN BY STEFANIE JAPEL

skills casting on, knit stitch, purl stitch, joining new yarn, binding off, seaming, weaving in ends

Want to pamper your favorite paperback? These soft book covers slip over the book or diary of your choice. There are two styles to choose from—a smooth cover knit with regular yarn (shown on the right) and a soft, furry one (shown on the left). This pattern fits a pocket paperback, but you can measure any book and adjust the pattern as needed.

measurements

Unfinished panel: 15 x 6¾ inches
Finished book cover: 4 x 6¾ inches

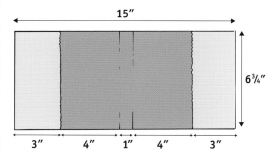

materials

For the smooth cover shown on the right:

* [Color 1] 1 skein of Lana Grossa Dito [60% cotton, 40% acrylic; 135m per 50g skein] (Color used here: 16)
* [Color 2] 1 skein of Lana Grossa Dito [60% cotton, 40% acrylic; 135m per 50g skein] (Color used here: 4)

  (Note: If you'd like to keep things simple, knit the whole thing in one color. Just get 2 skeins of whichever color you pick.)

For the fuzzy cover shown on the left:

* [Color 1] 2 skeins of Lana Grossa Pep [80% microfiber, 20% polyamide; 110m per 50g skein] (Color used here: 54)
* [Color 2] 1 skein of Lana Grossa Dito [60% cotton, 40% acrylic; 135m per 50g skein] (Color used here: 4)

For both covers:

* 1 pair size 5 (3.75mm) straight needles
* Ruler
* Row counter
* Tapestry needle

gauge

Regular yarn: 22 stitches/28 rows = 4 inches in stockinette stitch
Fuzzy yarn: 16 stitches/20 rows = 4 inches in stockinette stitch

pattern

The book cover is knit in one piece, then the ends are folded over and sewn to form the flaps.

Start the front flap:

* Cast on 38 stitches with Color 2.
* Knit 5 rows.
* Next row: Switch to stockinette stitch (knit 1 row, purl 1 row). Continue for 2¾ inches, ending with a purl row.

Now start the front:

* Change to Color 1 by joining a new ball of yarn (see page 26).
* Purl 1 row. This will help the book cover fold around the edge of the book.
* Work in stockinette stitch for 4 inches (or the width of the book's front cover). End with a purl row.
* Purl 1 more row.

Make the spine:

* Work in stockinette stitch for the width of the book's spine (usually about 1 inch), ending with a purl row.

Start the back cover:

* Purl 1 row. This is the start of the back cover.
* Work in stockinette stitch for 4 inches (or the width of the book's back cover). End with a purl row.
* Purl 1 more row.

Make the back flap:

* Work in stockinette stitch for 2¾ inches.
* Switch back to Color 2. Knit 5 rows.
* Bind off.

finishing

Fold the side flaps over, as shown, and stitch them down on the top and bottom. Weave in any loose ends.

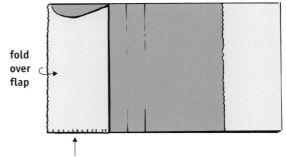

fold over flap

stitch to close top and bottom of flap

guys knit, too!

Anyone who says knitting is just for girls wasn't paying attention in history class! Ancient Egyptian men knit socks, Viking men did *naalbinding* (a simplified form of knitting still practiced today), and during the time of Queen Elizabeth I, British men knit millions of stockings for export all over Europe. Sailors and merchants spread the art of knitting around the Mediterranean; and in 1527, the first professional knitter's guild (men only!) started in Paris.

The number of guys who knit has grown steadily in the past few decades, too. Guys knit for the same reasons as girls, from wanting to make their own cool clothes to enjoying its relaxing side effects. Even cooler: guys who knit can make their own sweaters, and you can avoid the Sweater Curse!

The Sweater Curse is a popular knitters' myth that many argue is no joke. It says that if you knit a sweater for your boyfriend, you'll break up. (Do an online search for "sweater curse" and you'll read countless breakup stories blaming an innocent heap of yarn.) The only way to avoid the curse is to wait until a few years after you're married to knit a sweater for your husband.

In the meantime, teach your boyfriend to knit! He can make his own sweater—plus, there's nothing in the curse that says he can't knit you one!

Furry Denim Jacket Collar

PATTERN BY SHANNON OKEY

skills casting on, knit stitch, joining yarn, binding off, weaving in ends, sewing

Everyone has a jean jacket—make yours stand out with this cool, fuzzy collar. It uses two novelty yarns together—a "suede" and a "fuzzy-lump" yarn. Use these, or experiment with other novelty yarns to see what you like. If the 20-stitch width given in the directions is not wide enough to cover your entire collar, you'll know after knitting only a few rows. Just start over, casting on a few more stitches, about 25 or so.

size
One size fits all.

finished measurements
Approximately 16 x 4 inches but will vary according to the size of your jacket collar.

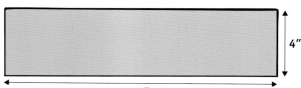

materials
* [Color 1] 1 skein of Lion Brand Suede [100% polyester; 122 yds per 85g skein] (Color used here: Teal)
* [Color 2] 1 skein of Lion Brand Fancy Fur [55% polyamide, 45% polyester; 39 yds per 50g skein] (Color used here: Night & Day)
* 1 pair size 10 (6mm) needles
* Ruler
* Tapestry needle
* Sewing needle and thread that matches the yarn

gauge
20 stitches/25 rows = 4 inches in stockinette stitch with both yarns held together

pattern
* Cast on 20 stitches with Color 1.
* At the start of the next row, join in Color 2 as if you were joining a new ball of yarn (see page 26). You'll then start knitting with both yarns held together.
* Knit in garter stitch (knit every row) until the piece is long enough to cover your jacket's collar (mine measured 16 inches).
* Stop knitting with Color 2 and cut the tail, leaving a few inches to weave in. Bind off using Color 1 only.

finishing
Weave in any loose ends. Lay the knitted collar over your jean jacket collar and use a sewing needle and thread to stitch it down along all four sides.

Needling Around

After you've been knitting a little while, you'll start to accumulate lots of knitting needles. Mine get together late at night and plan to take over the house, I think. So, to keep them in their place, I make needle cases. They're easy and fun, and a great gift for fellow knitters.

HERE'S HOW TO MAKE ONE:

1. Iron your fabric flat, with the printed side down. Fold over ½ inch along three sides and iron down.

2. Place the ironed fabric on a table with the printed side down and the unfolded edge on top. Fold the top edge down 9 inches.

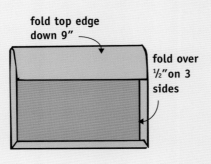

fold top edge down 9"

fold over ½" on 3 sides

3. Fold the bottom edge up 9 inches, overlapping the top edge by 2 inches. Make sure the folds are straight, then iron the piece again to set the folds.

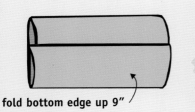

fold bottom edge up 9"

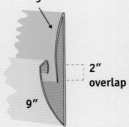

9"

9"

2" overlap

4. Now you're going to make the pockets for each set of needles. Take a pair of needles and stick them into the large bottom flap to see how wide each pocket should be. Mark where the pockets should be with pins or tailor's chalk.

5. Sew down the left and right sides first, to make side seams. Then sew each pocket seam, following the marks you made. Sew from the bottom edge up to the top of the flap.

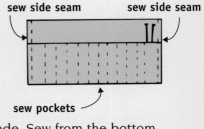

sew side seam

sew side seam

sew pockets

6. Put your knitting needles inside the pockets. There are two ways you can close the case: roll it up like a big cylinder, or fold it over itself from side to side, forming a flat case like an envelope. When you've decided which style you prefer, sew a button on the body side of the case and a matching piece of ribbon or elastic on the case edge. Or do it the easy way and just slip a hair scrunchie over the cylinder to keep it closed!

CYLINDER

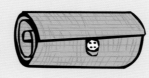

FLAT "ENVELOPE"

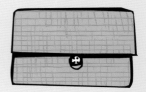

YOU WILL NEED:

* 1 square yard of heavy cotton fabric
* Sewing needle and matching thread
* Iron and ironing board
* Straight pins or tailor's chalk
* Yardstick, ruler, or measuring tape
* 1 button
* 3-inch scrap of yarn, narrow ribbon, or elastic

getting in shape

Time to get in shape…without even breaking a sweat! Rectangles are perfectly good for some things, but if you want to knit something that gets wider or narrower in just the right places, you need to learn how to increase and decrease.

HOW to INCREASE

When you want your knit object to become wider, you need to add stitches, or increase. There are three simple ways to increase, and all three are used in this book.

Make 1

The easiest way to increase is called **make 1** (often abbreviated as **m1**).

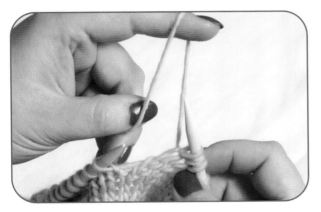

1 With your left finger, make a loop of yarn (twist it toward you).

2 Place the loop on the right-hand needle.

3 There, you've added a stitch!

web

Have a question about increasing and decreasing? Go to **www.knitgrrl.com!**

Knit Through Front and Back Loop

Another way to add a stitch is called knit through front and back loop (abbreviated as k1fb). This is almost like a regular knit stitch.

1 Place your needle in the loop and wrap the yarn around, just like a knit stitch.

2 Pull the stitch through toward you, again as if you were knitting, but don't pull it off the needle yet.

3 Take your right-hand needle and go around the left-hand needle to the back of the loop you just knit through.

4 Place the needle through the back loop and wrap the yarn around it.

5 Pull it through (this part is a little awkward at first; you need to angle your hands a bit).

6 Slip both new stitches off the needle.

Cable Cast-on

The cable cast-on is used to add on stitches in the middle of a row, and also to cast on when you want a firm edge at the beginning of your knitting.

1 Start with a slipknot, leaving a tail just a few inches long.

2 Insert your needles into the slipknot as if it were a regular stitch and begin to knit it.

3 Instead of pulling the stitch off your left-hand needle and onto the right, pull the new loop through to the front and place it on the tip of the left-hand needle.

tip Use a cable cast-on when you're low on yarn—it uses less yarn than the long-tail cast-on.

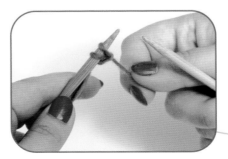

4 You've just made a new stitch. Now repeat steps 2–3, but insert your needle into the new stitch instead of the slipknot. Keep repeating steps 2–3 until you have the required number of stitches on your needle.

HOW to DECREASE

When you want your knit object to get narrower, you have to subtract stitches, or decrease. There are a few different ways to decrease stitches. Usually the first decreases you learn are knit 2 together and purl 2 together.

Knit 2 Together

When you are on a knit row, one of the easiest ways to decrease is to knit 2 together (abbreviated as k2tog).

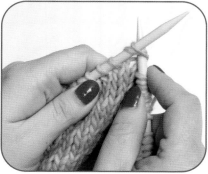

tip If you're having trouble doing k2tog, it might be because you are knitting too tightly. Try knitting a bit looser and see if it helps!

1 Place your right-hand needle through the next two stitches on the left-hand needle knitwise (that is, from front to back).

2 Wrap the yarn around the needle, as for a normal knit stitch.

3 Pull the needle through and slide both stitches off.

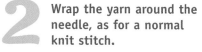

Purl 2 Together

To decrease when you are on a purl row, you **purl 2 together** (abbreviated as **p2tog**).

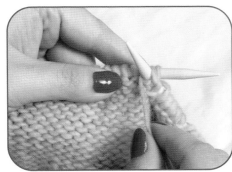

1 Place your right-hand needle through the next two stitches on the left-hand needle purlwise (from back to front).

2 Wrap the yarn around the needle, as for a normal purl stitch.

3 Pull the needle through and slide both stitches off.

Knit 2 Together Through Back Loop

Another way to decrease is **knit 2 stitches together through the back loop** (abbreviated as **k2tog tbl**). This creates a decrease that slants to the left.

1 Put the right-hand needle through the back loops of the next two stitches on the left-hand needle.

2 Wrap the yarn around the needle, as for a normal knit stitch.

3 Pull the wrap through and slide both stitches off.

Slip, Slip, Knit

Slip, slip, knit (abbreviated as SSK) is another type of decrease that slants to the left.

1 "Slip" one stitch from the left-hand needle to the right purlwise. To do this, insert the needle into the stitch, from right to left, and pull it off.

2 Slip a second stitch the same way.

3 Now insert your left-hand needle into the front of the two stitches you just slipped. Wrap your yarn around the back and complete like a regular knit stitch.

Slip 1, Knit 1, Pass Slipped Stitch Over

The last type of decrease used in this book is slip 1, knit 1, pass slipped stitch over (abbreviated as SKP).

1 "Slip" one stitch from the left-hand needle to the right knitwise. To do this, insert the needle as if you were making a knit stitch, but slide it off onto the needle without actually knitting it.

2 Knit the next stitch as usual, and slip it off the left-hand needle.

3 Insert the left-hand needle into the front of the slipped stitch on right-hand needle.

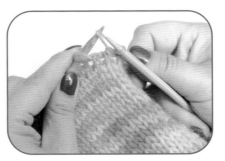 

4 Bring the slipped stitch over the knit stitch and off the right-hand needle, as if you were binding off.

Blossom Headband/Choker

finished measurements

15 x 1½ inches (without ties)

15"   1½

materials

For the headband:

* 1 skein of Cascade 220 [100% wool; 220 yds per 100g ball] (Color used here: 8888)
* 1 pair size 7 (4.5mm) needles

For the flowers:

* About 35 yards per flower of Cascade 220 [100% wool; 220 yds per 100g ball] (Colors used here: 9433 and 8114)
* 2 size 7 (4.5mm) double-pointed needles
* Sewing needle and thread to match the yarn
* Beads or small buttons
* Straight pins

For both:

* Ruler
* Tapestry needle

gauge

24 stitches/30 rows = 4 inches in stockinette stitch (Note: The headband is knit with smaller needles for a tighter gauge than suggested on the yarn label to minimize its stretch.)

pattern

* Make a slipknot, leaving a 12-inch tail, and slip it onto your needle.
* Row 1: K1fb. You now have 2 stitches.
* Row 2: K1fb, knit 1. Repeat this row 5 more times. You now have 8 stitches.
* Knit even (without increasing) for 10 to 12 inches, or until the piece stretches from one earlobe to the other.

PATTERN BY JENNA ADORNO

skills casting on, knit stitch, increasing (k1fb), decreasing (k2tog), weaving in ends

Find your inner flirt with this funky, flowery headband! The actual headband is simple to make, and you can add flowers, sew on beads or ribbon, or just leave it plain. It ties at the back, so you can wear it as a choker, too. Make the flowers from contrasting color yarn, or yarn left over from other projects.

* Next row: K2tog, knit 4, k2tog. You now have 6 stitches.
* Next row: K2tog, knit 2, k2tog. You now have 4 stitches.
* Next row: K2tog twice. You now have only 2 stitches.
* Next row: K2tog. You now have 1 stitch left.
* Cut a 12-inch tail and thread it through the last stitch, but do not pull it tight yet.

finishing

1. To make the ties, cut a 24-inch piece of yarn (the same color as the headband). Pull it halfway through the last stitch, creating 2 tails. Now pull the last stitch tight— you should end up with 3 even 12-inch tails. Braid the 3 strands of yarn (see page 89) and knot the ends.

2. Cut another 24-inch piece of yarn to make a tail at the other end. Use a tapestry needle to thread it through the first slipknot and pull it halfway through, creating 3 tails. Braid the 3 strands of yarn and knot the ends.

braided tie   **braided tie**

3. Weave in any loose ends. To make the flowers, see page 90.

blocking

Blocking is a way of arranging damp knitted things to dry so they will retain their shape or, if the shape wasn't quite right, to help you shape them more to your liking.

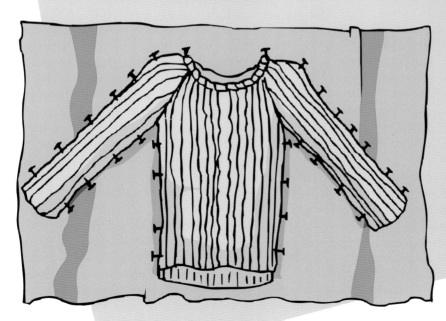

For small pieces such as the Striped Pencil Purse on page 48, pin the pieces down on an ironing board and spray them with water from a squirt bottle. You can also block them using steam from an iron, but do not touch the iron to your knitting! Allow the pieces to dry completely before removing them from the ironing board.

For a larger item such as a sweater, wet it thoroughly and remove all excess water by rolling it in a towel. Arrange the item on a towel or sweater rack and pin it into the position you want. Allow it to dry thoroughly.

Striped Pencil Purse

PATTERN BY KIMBERLI MACKAY

skills casting on, knit stitch, purl stitch, joining yarn, make 1, binding off, seaming, weaving in ends

This cute little buttoned purse can be used to hold pens, makeup, odds and ends in your locker—whatever! To make the striped pattern, you just alternate colors. Knit with one color for two rows, then let go of that color and pick up the new one, letting the first yarn "dangle" until you're ready to use it again.

measurements

Unfinished main piece:
9 x 14 inches
Finished purse:
9 x 4 x 2 inches

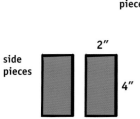

materials

* [Color 1] 1 skein of Brown Sheep Cotton Fleece [80% cotton, 20% Merino Wool, 215 yds per 100g skein] (Color used here: Wolverine Blue)
* [Color 2] 1 skein of Brown Sheep Cotton Fleece [80% cotton, 20% Merino Wool, 215 yds per 100g skein] (Color used here: Malibu Blue)
* 1 pair size 6 (4mm) needles
* Row counter
* Tapestry needle
* Straight pins
* 3 1¼-inch buttons
* Sewing needle and thread to match yarn

gauge

20 stitches/26 rows = 4 inches in stockinette stitch

pattern

The pattern is knit in three pieces—one big striped piece that you fold over to make the main body and two smaller side pieces that you attach later.

Begin at the top:
* Cast on 47 stitches with Color 1.
* Row 1: Knit.
* Row 2: Purl.
* Now drop Color 1 but do not cut it, and join Color 2.
* Row 3: Knit with Color 2.
* Row 4: Purl with Color 2.
* Now drop Color 2 but do not cut it, and pick up Color 1.
* This establishes the stripe pattern. Repeat Rows 1–4 twice more for a total of 6 stripes (3 of each color).

Now start the front:

* Rows 13–14: Knit 2 rows with Color 1. This creates a purl ridge on the right (public) side.
* Rows 15–36: Go back to making stripes in stockinette stitch until there are 6 stripes of each color on the front and 9 stripes of each color total, ending with Color 2.

Start the bottom:

* Rows 37–38: Knit 2 rows with Color 1. This creates a purl ridge on the right side.
* Rows 39–52: Continue stripes in stockinette stitch for 14 more rows, ending with a stripe in Color 2.

Start the back:

* Rows 53–54: Knit 2 rows with Color 1. This creates a purl ridge on the right side.
* Rows 55–76: Continue stripes in stockinette stitch, ending with Color 2. There should be 12 stripes on the back (6 of each color, including the purl ridges).

Make the buttonhole flap:

* Rows 77–78: Knit 2 rows with Color 1. This creates a purl ridge on the right side.
* Row 79: Knit with Color 1.
* Row 80: Purl with Color 1.
* Row 81: Knit with Color 2.
* Row 82: Purl with Color 2.
* Row 83 (buttonhole row): Knit 4, bind off 3, knit 15, bind off 3, knit 15, bind off 3, knit 4.
* Row 84: Purl 4, add 3 stitches (using the make 1 method), purl 15, add 3 more using make 1 method, purl 15, add 3 more using make 1 method, purl 4.
* Row 85: Knit with Color 1.
* Row 86: Purl with Color 1.
* Row 87: Knit with Color 2.
* Bind off all stitches purlwise with Color 2 (see "tip," below).

> ## tip
> Binding off purlwise is just like regular binding off, but in a purl row. Purl two stitches, then lift the right-hand stitch over the left. Purl the next stitch, slip the right-hand stitch over, and so on.

Side pieces (make 2)

* Cast on 14 stitches with Color 1.
* Row 1: Knit.
* Row 2: Purl.
* Repeat these 2 rows 11 more times. You will have knit 24 rows.
* Bind off.

finishing

1. Weave in any loose ends and block the pieces.

2. To attach the side pieces, lay the main piece down, right side up. Lay the side pieces, right sides down, on top of it with the edges aligned, as shown.

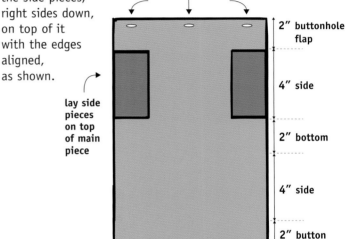

lay side pieces on top of main piece

buttonholes

2" buttonhole flap
4" side
2" bottom
4" side
2" button flap

main piece

3. Pin one side piece to the main body, folding the body around to form the purse. Keep pinning the side piece all the way around. Repeat for the other side.

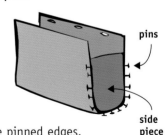

pins

side piece

4. Seam the side pieces along the pinned edges. Weave in any loose ends. Turn the bag right side out.

5. To figure out where to put the buttons, fold the top flap over and then fold the buttonhole flap over that. Push a pin through each buttonhole down into the flap below. Open both flaps and sew a button onto the top flap at each pin.

Workout Water-Bottle Holder

PATTERN BY KERRIE ALLMAN

skills casting on, knit stitch, purl stitch, yarn over (see page 57), decreasing (k2tog), binding off, seaming, weaving in ends

Next time you head out to yoga, dance class, or soccer practice, bring along a bottle of water in this over-the-shoulder holder. Its mesh body, made using simple yarn overs (see page 57), is stretchy enough to accommodate most bottle sizes, and the seed stitch bottom is firm enough to support a full bottle. Drink up!

measurements

Unfinished body: 10 x 8 inches; base: 6 x 5 inches
Finished holder: Fits most water bottles 1 liter or smaller

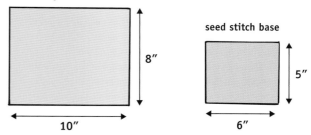

mesh body

8"

10"

seed stitch base

5"

6"

materials

* [Color 1] 2 skeins of Rowan Cotton Tape [100% cotton; 71 yds per 50g skein] (Color used here: 062 pink)
* [Color 2] 1 skein of Rowan Cotton Tape [100% cotton; 71 yds per 50g skein] (Color used here: 064 blue)
* 1 pair size 8 (5mm) needles
* Ruler
* Row counter
* Tapestry needle

gauge

16 stitches/24 rows = 4 inches in stockinette stitch

pattern

This pattern is knit in 2 pieces—the mesh body and the seed stitch base.

Mesh body

* Cast on 40 stitches with Color 1.
* Row 1: Knit.
* Row 2: Purl.
* Row 3 (begin mesh pattern stitch): Knit 1, *yarn over, k2tog* to last stitch, knit 1.
* Row 4: Purl.
* Repeat rows 3 and 4. Do this 14 more times or until work measures about 6 inches.
* Work 6 rows in stockinette stitch (knit 1 row, purl 1 row), ending with a purl row.

* Next row (eyelet row): Knit 1, *yarn over, k2tog* to last stitch, knit 1.
* Work 3 rows in stockinette stitch, starting and ending with a purl row.
* Next row (picot row): Knit 1, *yarn over, k2tog* to last stitch, knit 1.
* Work 3 rows in stockinette stitch, beginning and ending with a purl row.
* Bind off all stitches.

Seed stitch base
* Cast on 10 stitches with Color 2.
* Row 1: *Knit 1, purl 1* to end.
* Row 2: *Purl 1, knit 1* to end.
* Repeat these 2 rows for a total of 18 rows.
* Bind off.

finishing

1. At the top of the mesh body, fold down the last 3 rows of stockinette stitch to form a scalloped edge, and sew in place on the inside using a tapestry needle and matching yarn.

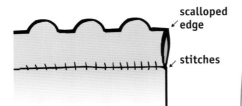

scalloped edge

stitches

2. With the right side on the inside, sew the side seam of the water bottle holder (see page 28) to form a cylinder. Turn it right side out.

3. To attach the base, first turn the corners of the base under. Using blue yarn and a tapestry needle, stitch it to the bottom of the cylinder, gathering the base to fit as you go.

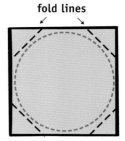

fold lines

4. To make the strap, cut a piece of Color 1 yarn 7 yards long. Fold in half and loop the folded end around a doorknob. Twist the free ends until the yarn is twisted all the way along. Remove the other end from the doorknob and allow the yarn to twist together from the middle. The twisted cord will measure about 65 inches.

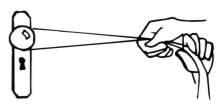

5. Attach the strap by threading the twisted cord through the eyelets and tying the ends of the cord together.

the seed stitch

The seed stitch is made by knitting one stitch, then moving your yarn between the needles so it's in the front, purling one stitch, moving the yarn to the back, knitting one stitch, and so on until one row is completed. On the next row, you knit where you purled, and purl where you knit, forming a checkerboard of knit and purl stitches. The seed stitch looks fancy, but it's very easy and is great for adding a little pizzazz to the bottom of a hat or scarf.

The seed stitch bottom supports the bottle while the mesh body stretches to accommodate different bottle sizes.

Beauty-to-Go Bag

PATTERN BY KIMBERLI MACKAY

skills casting on, knit stitch, purl stitch, decreasing (k2tog, p2tog), binding off, seaming, weaving in ends

Need a way to organize your lip gloss? You need this bag! What's even better is that you can make at least two bags from one skein of yarn—Hello, birthday present idea for your best friend!

measurements

Unfinished main piece:
6 ½ x 16 ½ inches

Finished purse:
6 ½ x 5 x 2 ½ inches

side pieces   2½"   5"

main piece   6½"   16½"

materials

* 1 skein of Brown Sheep Cotton Fleece [80% cotton, 20% wool; 215 yards per 100g skein] (Color used here: CW-810 Cherry Moon)
* 1 pair size 6 (4mm) needles
* Row counter
* Tapestry needle
* Straight pins
* 2 1-inch buttons
* Sewing needle and thread to match yarn

gauge

22 stitches/36 rows = 4 inches in stockinette

pattern

This pattern is knit in three pieces—one long piece that you fold over to make the main body and two smaller side pieces that you attach later.

Begin the front:
* Cast on 32 stitches.
* Row 1: Knit.
* Row 2: Purl.
* Repeat rows 1 and 2 until you have 30 rows.

Now start the bottom:
* Row 31: Purl.
* Row 32: *Knit 1, purl 1* to end.
* Row 33: *Purl 1, knit 1* to end.
* Rows 34–43: Repeat rows 32 and 33. Do this 5 times. (You will have 12 rows in seed stitch.)
* Row 44: Knit.

Start the back:

* Rows 45–74: Work in stockinette stitch (knit 1 row, purl 1 row), as you did for the front of the bag.

Knit the front flap:

* Row 75: Purl.
* Row 76: *Knit 1, purl 1* to end.
* Row 77: *Purl 1, knit 1* to end.
* Rows 78–93: Repeat rows 76 and 77. Do this 8 times. (You will have 19 rows in all for the flap.)
* Bind off.

Side pieces (make 2)

* Cast on 12 stitches.
* Row 1: Knit.
* Row 2: Purl.
* Rows 3–8: Repeat rows 1 and 2. Do this 3 more times.
* Row 9: K2tog, knit to end.
* Row 10: P2tog, purl to end. You should have 10 stitches.
* Row 11: Knit.
* Row 12: Purl.
* Rows 13–18: Repeat rows 11 and 12. Do this 3 more times.
* Row 19: K2tog, knit to end.
* Row 20: P2tog, purl to end. You should have 8 stitches.
* Rows 21: Knit.
* Row 22: Purl.
* Rows 23–26: Repeat rows 21 and 22. Do this 2 more times.
* Row 27: K2tog, knit to end.
* Row 28: P2tog, purl to end. You now have 6 stitches.
* Row 29: Knit.
* Row 30: Purl.
* Row 31: K2tog, knit to end.
* Row 32: P2tog, purl to end. You should have 4 stitches.
* Row 33: Knit.
* Row 34: Purl.
* Row 35: K2tog, knit to end.
* Row 36: P2tog, purl to end.
* Row 37: K2tog. Cut the end and pull the tail through the last stitch.

Button loops (make 2)

* Knit two 2¾-inch pieces of i-cord (see page 90).

finishing

1. Block all the pieces (see page 47).

2. Lay the main piece flat on a table, right side up. Place one side piece, right side down, on top of the main piece. Make sure that you align its cast-on edge with the beginning of the bottom seed stitch section. Pin into place. Repeat with the other side piece.

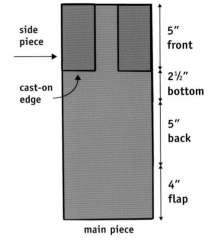

3. Now fold the body around to form the purse, pinning all the way around until you reach the beginning of the flap.

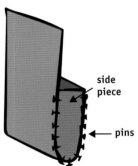

4. Sew the seam with yarn and a tapestry needle. Weave in any loose ends. Turn right side out.

5. Fold the flap down. Sew the buttons on just below the flap and 1 inch in from the sides.

6. Use a straight pin to mark the center of each button on the edge of the flap. This will be your guide for placing the i-cord buttonholes.

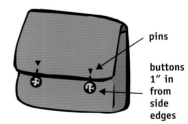

7. Bring the ends of one piece of i-cord together, creating a loop. Stitch the i-cord ends securely to the underside of the flap at the pin. Repeat with the other i-cord.

it's a pick-up

Ready to learn something new? This chapter teaches you how to pick up stitches from the edge of an item you've already knit. It's as easy as casting on new stitches, and can be used to make lots of cool things!

PICKING up STITCHES

The patterns in this chapter ask you to pick up stitches from a finished edge—for example, to add a tie to a belt or a kerchief. Here's how to do it.

1 Insert the left-hand needle into a stitch on one edge of your knitting (the pattern will tell you which edge).

2 Insert the right-hand needle behind it, as if it were a stitch already on the needle and you were about to knit it.

3 Knit the stitch as if you were joining new yarn (see page 26).

4 Slide the completed stitch off the left-hand needle.

Repeat steps 1–4 with the next stitch on the finished edge, moving to the left. Keep picking up stitches, working from right to left, until you have the number indicated in the pattern.

Boho Belt

PATTERN BY MEGAN REARDON

skills casting on, knit stitch, purl stitch, yarn over, decreasing (k2tog), picking up stitches, binding off

Add some excitement to your jeans-and-a-tee look with this Boho Belt in eye-popping orange (or whatever shade you like). You'll go from shy girl to fly girl in no time! If you want to put a little jingle into your walk, tie charms to the ends. The belt is too long to knit on straight needles, so the pattern uses circular needles, which are longer—one of many reasons to use circulars, even for patterns knit flat!

size

S (M, L)
Decide how long you want your belt to be and pick one of the sizes below. (All three sizes are 2 inches wide—only the length changes.)
Small: 2 x 32 inches
Medium: 2 x 34 inches
Large: 2 x 36 inches

materials

* 1 skein of Lion Brand Cotton-Ease [50% cotton, 50% acrylic; 207 yds per 100g ball] (Color used here: Orangeade)
* 1 24- or 36-inch size 10 (6mm) circular needle
* 1 size 11 (8mm) circular needle, any length
* 1 pair size 6 (4mm) straight needles
* Ruler
* Row counter
* Tapestry needle
* Small charms (optional)

gauge

16 stitches/30 rows = 4 inches in garter stitch (unstretched)

pattern

* Cast on 85 (90, 95) stitches with the size 10 circular needle. (You'll need a tail 9–10 feet long to cast on!)
* Row 1: Knit.
* Row 2: *Knit 5, yarn over* to last 5 stitches, then knit 5.
* Row 3: Knit 3, k2tog, *knit 4, k2tog* to last 6 stitches, then knit 6.
* Row 4: Knit.
* Repeat rows 1–4 twice more.
* Bind off using the size 11 needle. (This will allow for stretch in the belt while still creating a firm edge.)

tip

This pattern has instructions for multiple sizes. The first number refers to the smallest size, and the numbers inside the parentheses refer to the other sizes. Use only the number for the size you want. It helps to photocopy the pattern and go through it first, highlighting only the numbers for your size to avoid confusion.

Ties

* Lay the belt flat, right side up. Using size 6 straight needles, pick up 7 stitches along one end of the belt.
* Next row: Bind off 1, knit to last stitch, bind off the last stitch.

* Next row: Knit 5.
* Next row: Bind off 1, knit 3, bind off the last stitch.
* Next row: Knit 3.
* Next row: Knit 1, bind off the last 2 stitches together.
* Cut the yarn, leaving a 21-inch tail, and pull it through the last stitch, but do not pull tight.
* Repeat on the other end of the belt.

finishing

1. Cut several 42-inch pieces of yarn. Pull them halfway through the last stitch, leaving tails of equal lengths. (You can add more or less fringe according to your preference.) Pull the bound-off loop tight.

2. Repeat on the other end of the belt.

3. If you want to personalize your belt, tie charms to the ends of the fringe.

yo! here's how to do a yarn over

A yarn over, or YO, creates a decorative hole (or eyelet) in the knitted fabric. To make one, just bring the yarn to the front between stitches by drawing it through the space between the two needles, crossing it over the top of the right-hand needle, and bringing it back to where it was. Then insert the needle into the next loop on the left-hand needle and continue as with a normal stitch. The extra wrap will disappear when you knit the next row, forming a hole.

Glo-Girl Kerchief

PATTERN BY MEGAN REARDON

skills cable cast-on, knit stitch, purl stitch, yarn over, decreasing (k2tog, SSK), picking up stitches, binding off

This funky kerchief goes hand in hand with the Boho Belt. You can even make both projects from one ball of yarn!

size
One size fits all.

measurements
14 x 8 inches
(unstretched, without ties)

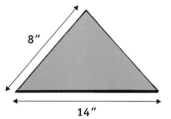

materials
* 1 skein of Lion Brand Cotton-Ease [50% cotton, 50% acrylic; 207 yds per 100g ball] (Color used here: Orangeade)
* 1 pair size 10 (6mm) needles
* 1 pair size 6 (4mm) needles
* Row counter
* Tapestry needle

gauge
16 stitches/30 rows = 4 inches in garter stitch

pattern
* Cast on 45 stitches with the size 10 needles using cable cast-on (see page 41). This will provide a firm edge.
* Row 1: Knit.
* Row 2: *Knit 5, yarn over* to last 5 stitches, then knit 5.
* Row 3: Knit 3, k2tog, *knit 4, k2tog* to last 6 stitches, then knit 6.
* Row 4: Knit.
* Repeat rows 1–4 twice more.
* Row 13 (right side): Knit 1, SSK, knit to last 3 stitches, k2tog, knit 1.
* Row 14: Knit.
* Repeat rows 13 and 14 until you have only 7 stitches left.
* Next row: With right side facing you, knit 1, SSK, knit 1, k2tog, knit 1.

* Next row: Knit.
* Next row: SSK, knit 1, k2tog.
* Next row: Knit.
* Bind off the last 3 stitches.

Ties
* Hold the kerchief with the right side facing you. Using size 6 needles, pick up 7 stitches along one edge of the top band.
* Next row: Bind off 1, knit to last stitch, bind off the last stitch.
* Next row: Knit 5.
* Next row: Bind off 1, knit 3, bind off the last stitch.
* Next row: Knit 3.
* Next row: Knit 1, bind off the last 2 stitches together.
* Cut the yarn, leaving a 21-inch tail, and pull it through the last stitch, but do not pull tight.
* Cut a 42-inch piece of yarn and pull it halfway through the last stitch, leaving 3 equal tails. Pull the bound-off loop tight. Braid the 3 strands (see page 89).
* Repeat on the other side.

Juicy Journaling

Do you have a collection of loose patterns you bought at a yarn store? Want to keep track of the yarns used in your favorite scarf? (Even the best knitters can forget a certain yarn or color name months after they've knit it.) Need a place to keep yarn labels so you can refer back to the care instructions? Then you need a knit journal!

HERE'S HOW TO MAKE ONE:

1. Measure the size of the window opening on the cover. You're going to knit a panel to go behind this window. Knit a rectangle that is at least 1 inch longer and wider than the window—2 inches if the yarn isn't very stretchy.

2. Most albums will have a piece of paper behind the window on the inside of the front cover. Remove this paper so you can see the clear window.

3. Lay the knitted panel on the inside front cover, behind the window opening. Secure it along all four sides using packing tape.

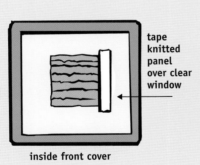

tape knitted panel over clear window

inside front cover

4. Iron the lining fabric flat. Fold under ½ inch along each side and iron down.

5. Place the lining fabric on the inside front cover of your album, right side up, on top of the knitted panel. Glue it down along all four edges. Let the glue dry.

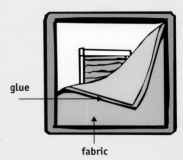

glue

fabric

FINISHED JOURNAL

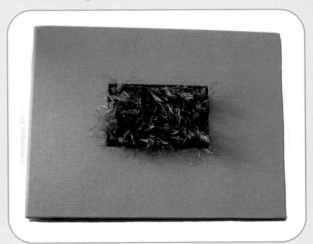

YOU WILL NEED:

* A photo album with a cut-out window on the front cover
* Piece of fabric 1 inch larger than the album cover
* Yarn scraps from other projects
* Knitting needles (any size)
* Ruler
* Iron and ironing board
* Packing tape
* Clear glue (such as Elmer's)

Striped
Cardigan

PATTERN BY KRISTI PORTER

skills casting on, knit stitch, cable cast-on, picking up stitches, yarn over, decreasing (k2tog), binding off, weaving in ends

This cardigan looks much more complicated than it is—it's knit in a self-striping yarn, so the stripes happen automatically! Cool, huh? You can, of course, make the sweater in a plainer yarn if you want (see the tip about the correct gauge at right). The pattern gives instructions for five sizes, and since the sweater fits pretty snugly, choose a bigger size if you're unsure. It's helpful to photocopy the pattern and highlight only the numbers for your size before starting.

size

XS (S, M, L, XL)

Size	Width around chest	Length
XS	30 inches	16 inches
S	32 inches	17 inches
M	34 inches	17½ inches
L	36 inches	18 inches
XL	38 inches	19 inches

materials

* 7 (8, 9, 10, 10) skeins of Noro Kureyon yarn [100% wool; 109 yds per 50g skein] (Color used here: 138)
* 1 pair size 8 (5mm) needles (or size needed to match gauge)
* Row counter
* Ruler
* Tapestry needle
* 5 (6, 6, 6, 6) 1-inch buttons
* Sewing needle and thread to match buttons

gauge

14 stitches/28 rows = 4 inches in garter stitch (Note: If you are substituting yarns, look for one that lists its gauge as 18 stitches/24 rows = 4 inches in stockinette stitch.)

tip Getting your gauge right is important when you are knitting something that really has to fit. Being even just half a stitch off is enough to make your sweater fit badly! Take the time to check your gauge with a swatch (see page 30) and you'll be happier in the long run.

pattern

You'll knit the body of the sweater from side to side, starting with the right front, then the back, then the left front. The bottom of the sweater will be straight. The other end will go in and out as you make the armholes and neck opening. You'll then pick up stitches along the armholes and knit the sleeves from the shoulder down. Always cast on and bind off on the same end of the knitted piece.

main body

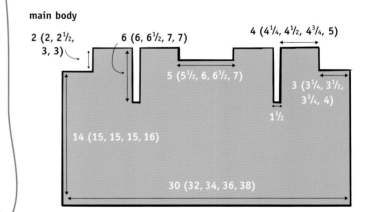

tip Keep a ruler handy because lengths are given in rows *and* inches. Counting the number of rows (or counting two rows for each garter ridge) will assure that the shoulder flaps match up. It's also a good idea to measure as you go.

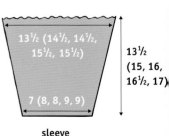

sleeve

Main body

Start with the right front:

* Cast on 49 (53, 53, 53, 55) stitches.

* Knit 21 (23, 25, 27, 29) rows. The piece should now measure 3 (3$\frac{1}{4}$, 3$\frac{1}{2}$, 3$\frac{3}{4}$, 4) inches.

* Cast on an additional 7 (7, 9, 11, 11) stitches using the cable cast-on. This will be the neck edge. You will have 56 (60, 62, 64, 66) stitches.

* Knit 28 (30, 32, 34, 36) rows. The piece should measure 4 (4$\frac{1}{4}$, 4$\frac{1}{2}$, 4$\frac{3}{4}$, 5) inches from where you did the cable cast-on.

Shape the right armhole:

* Bind off 21 (23, 23, 25, 25) stitches at neck edge.

* Knit 10 rows (1$\frac{1}{2}$ inches) for the bottom of the armhole.

* Cast on 21 (23, 23, 25, 25) stitches at neck edge using cable cast-on.

Knit the back:

* Knit 28 (30, 32, 34, 36) rows. The piece should measure 4 (4$\frac{1}{4}$, 4$\frac{1}{2}$, 4$\frac{3}{4}$, 5) inches from the armhole.

* Bind off 3 stitches at neck edge.

* Knit 36 (38, 42, 46, 48) rows. The piece measures 5 (5$\frac{1}{2}$, 6, 6$\frac{1}{2}$, 7) inches from where you bound off.

* Cast on 3 stitches at neck edge using cable cast-on.

* Knit 28 (30, 32, 34, 36) rows. The piece measures 4 (4$\frac{1}{4}$, 4$\frac{1}{2}$, 4$\frac{3}{4}$, 5) inches from last cast-on.

Shape the left armhole:

* Bind off 21 (23, 23, 25, 25) stitches at neck edge.

* Knit 10 rows (1$\frac{1}{2}$ inches) for the bottom of the armhole.

* Cast on 21 (23, 23, 25, 25) stitches at neck edge using cable cast-on.

Knit the left front:

* Knit 28 (30, 32, 34, 36) rows. The piece measures 4 (4$\frac{1}{4}$, 4$\frac{1}{2}$, 4$\frac{3}{4}$, 5) inches from the armhole.

* Bind off 7 (7, 9, 11, 11) stitches at neck edge. There should be 49 (53, 53, 53, 55) stitches on the needle.

* Knit 16 (18, 20, 22, 24) rows. The piece measures 2$\frac{1}{4}$ (2$\frac{1}{2}$, 3, 3$\frac{1}{4}$, 3$\frac{1}{2}$) inches from where you bound off.

* Next row (buttonhole row): Knit 3, *yarn over, k2tog, knit 7,* repeat from * 5 (6, 6, 6, 6) times, then knit 8 (3, 3, 3, 5).

* Knit 4 more rows.

* Bind off all stitches loosely—using a larger size needle if necessary.

Sleeves

* The completed body has two U-shapes that form the armholes. Beginning at one shoulder edge and working on the right (public) side, pick up 47 (51, 51, 55, 55) stitches—21 (23, 23, 25, 25) from each side where you bound off or cast on and 5 from the bottom of the U.

* Knit back and forth in garter stitch, decreasing (k2tog) 1 stitch at each side every 8th row 11 (12, 12, 12, 12) times. You should have 25 (27, 27, 31, 31) stitches.

* Knit even (without increasing or decreasing) until the sleeve measures 13$\frac{1}{2}$ (15, 16, 16$\frac{1}{2}$, 17) inches from the underarm (or the right length for your arms when you try it on).

* Bind off all stitches.

* Repeat for second sleeve.

finishing

1. Lay the sweater flat with right sides together and sew each sleeve together from shoulder to wrist. This seam will go along the top of your arm. Turn right side out.

2. To place the buttons on the front, lay the sweater flat and place the buttonhole edge on top of the plain edge. Push a pin through each buttonhole down into the plain edge to mark the right spot. Sew on a button at each pin.

tip If you knit your sweater in Noro Kureyon yarn, you *must* hand wash it.

Full-of-Holes Scarf

PATTERN BY KIRSTEN ZERBINIS

skills casting on, cable cast-on, knit stitch, yarn over, increasing (make 1), decreasing (SKP), picking up stitches, binding off, weaving in ends

Have ya heard? Scarves aren't just for winter anymore! Flip this lacy scarf over your shoulder for a quick pick-me-up. Or pin the two corners together and wear it as a summery mini-capelet. It's a good idea to make the tassels for the ends first, so you'll be sure to have enough yarn to finish the project. For a closer view, check out the photo opposite the table of contents.

finished measurements

6 feet x 5 inches

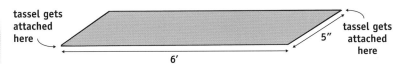

tassel gets attached here

tassel gets attached here

5"

6'

materials

* 2 skeins of Koigu Premium Painters' Palette Merino [100% merino wool; 170 yds per 50g skein] (Color used here: p211)
* 1 pair size 6 (4mm) needles
* Ruler
* Row counter
* Tapestry needle

gauge

18 stitches/24 rows = 4 inches in stockinette stitch

pattern

* Cast on 55 stitches.
* Rows 1–4: Knit.
* Row 5: Bind off 5, knit 1, *bind off 6, knit 3,* repeat from * 4 times, then bind off 6, knit 1, then cast on 5 stitches using cable cast-on. You'll have 2 stitches together at either side and groups of 4 stitches in the middle.
* Note: On the next row, you will decrease 1 stitch on the right edge of each hole and pick up an extra stitch from the left edge of each hole in the row below. This technique gives the holes cleaner edges.

* Row 6: Knit 5, *SKP, cast on 6 stitches tightly using cable cast-on, then create a 7th new stitch by picking up 1 stitch from the left side of the hole, knit 2.* Repeat from * to * until the end of the row.
* Repeat rows 1–6 until the scarf is desired length, ending with row 4.
* Bind off.

finishing

Weave in ends. Block the scarf (see page 47). Make two 3-inch tassels following the directions on page 89. Then tie a tassel to each point.

tip To "slip" a stitch means to move it from one needle to the other without knitting or doing anything to it—simple!

just bead it

So now you've got the hang of knitting, right? Ready to add a little sparkle? This chapter will teach you how to knit with beads. You heard me—beads! Here we'll use them to make beautiful jewelry, but once you learn the basics it's easy to add them to any knitted project.

KNITTING with BEADS

Designer Sivia Harding is a master at working with beads, and she came up with the method we use here. Once you learn her basic steps, you can put beads anywhere—why not use them to trim a scarf or to create a border on a hat? The only limits are your imagination…and the beads you choose!

Stringing Beads onto Yarn

The first step is to get the beads onto your yarn so you can knit with them. This is called **stringing**, or **threading** the beads. You can use either dental floss or a large-eyed needle. The needle you choose has to have an eye large enough for the yarn to go through but be small enough to fit through the hole in the beads.

1 Double the dental floss over your yarn, then slide your beads onto the dental floss.

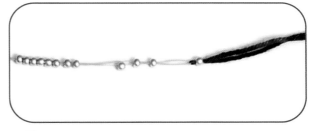

2 Slide the beads from the dental floss onto the yarn.

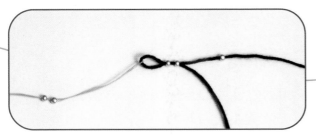

3 Once your beads are on the yarn, pull the short tail of yarn through so the beads are left on the working yarn only.

> **tip** Beads come in different sizes that will fit on different weight yarns. Seed beads are measured in numbers such as 6, 8, or 11. Size 6 (indicated like this: 6/0) will fit easily on fine yarn. With seed beads, the higher the number, the *smaller* the bead. Larger beads, including the faceted ones used here, are designated by their size (for example, a 6mm bead measures 6 millimeters). With these beads, the higher the number, the *larger* the bead.

Slip Bead

Once you've strung the beads onto the yarn, they're ready to be knitted into your project. **Slip bead** is the term for bringing the first bead up and knitting with it.

1 Bring your yarn in front of the needle, as if you were going to do a purl stitch. Slide the first bead strung onto the working yarn up close to the right-hand needle.

2 Slip one stitch purlwise (see page 85).

3 Move the yarn to the back, as if you were going to do a knit stitch. Leave the bead in front of the slipped stitch.

4 Knit the next stitch (or purl it, depending on what your pattern says). The bead should stay securely attached in front.

getting into the groove

When you've strung the beads onto your yarn and are ready to start knitting, push the beads a couple of feet away from you on the strand of yarn to give yourself room to knit. Keep pushing the beads away from you as you knit, sliding up one bead at a time as you need it. Some knitters like to keep a bowl nearby and let the beaded yarn, which can be quite heavy, fall loosely coiled into the bowl.

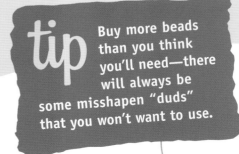

tip Buy more beads than you think you'll need—there will always be some misshapen "duds" that you won't want to use.

Place Bead

Sometimes a pattern will ask you to **place bead.** This means to get a new bead—one that *isn't* strung onto your yarn—and to insert it into the knitting using a crochet hook.

1 Slide a bead onto the crochet hook and insert the crochet hook into the stitch where you want the bead to go.

2 With the hook facing you, use your thumb to slide the bead right up next to the stitch.

3 Hook the stitch and pull it through the hole in the bead and off the knitting needle.

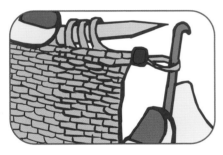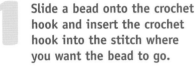

4 The bead should end up sitting at the base of the stitch.

other materials

In addition to the yarn and beads listed in each project, you will need the following tools:

* 2 size 4 double-pointed needles (Note: Bamboo or wood work best because the yarn does not slip as much on these needles.)
* 1 size B (or smaller) crochet hook for placing beads
* Dental floss or a large-eyed beading needle, for stringing beads onto yarn
* Row counter
* Several small stitch holders or small pieces of smooth yarn scraps for holding stitches
* Sharp scissors
* Sharp tapestry needle
* Fray Check (available in sewing stores) to keep yarn ends from fraying (optional)

5 Slide the stitch back onto the knitting needle and carefully withdraw the crochet hook.

Vintage Necklace

PATTERN BY SIVIA HARDING

skills   casting on, using double-pointed needles, knit stitch, purl stitch, increasing (make 1), decreasing (k2tog, p2tog) using a stitch holder, binding off, weaving in ends, i-cord

Get your retro vibe going with this beautiful necklace inspired by jewelry from the 1950s. Once upon a time, every teenaged girl or woman owned at least one multi-stranded pearl necklace. This updated version has strands of sparkly i-cord with a single button closure in the back.

finished measurements
12 inches around

materials
* 1 skein of Lang Opal (or Opal Color) [58% nylon, 42% viscose; 155m per 50g ball] (Color used here: variegated copper 15)
* 144 seed beads total: topaz size 6/0 and root beer size 3/0
* 1 8mm Czech glass bead for the closure
* 2 size 4 (3.5mm) double-pointed needles (DPNs)
* Stitch holder
See page 67 for additional tools needed.

gauge
32 stitches/48 rows = 4 inches in garter stitch
(Note: Exact gauge is not critical for this project.)

pattern
* String 42 beads onto the yarn with dental floss or a large-eyed beading needle. Push the beads down the yarn until you have 1 or 2 feet of unbeaded yarn free to work with.
* Cast on 3 stitches.
* Row 1: Knit 1 row. You will be using the DPNs just like regular straight needles.
* Row 2: Knit 1, make 1, knit 1, make 1, knit 1. You now have 5 stitches.

* Row 3: Purl 1, *knit 1, purl 1* to end of row.
* Row 4: Knit 1, purl 1, knit 1, make 1, make 1, purl 1, knit 1. You now have 7 stitches.
* Work in knit 1, purl 1 rib for 5 rows.
* Next row: Knit 1, purl 1, knit 1, purl 1, knit 1, make 1, make 1, purl 1, knit 1. You now have 9 stitches.
* Work in knit 1, purl 1 rib for 5 more rows.
* Next row: Purl, increasing (make 1) 3 stitches evenly across row. You will have 12 stitches.
* Next row: Knit 4. Slide the remaining 8 stitches from your needle onto a stitch holder (see page 70).

Begin i-cord:

* You'll now start knitting the i-cord (see page 90). Keep the needles in your same hands and do not turn the work. Push the stitches to the other end of the DPN. Bring the working yarn around the back of the work in preparation for knitting the next row.
* Next row: Knit 2, make 1, knit 2. You will have 5 stitches.
* Continue in i-cord from now on (do not turn work after each row).

Begin "slip bead" pattern:

* Row 1: Knit 2, slip bead, knit 2.
* Row 2: Knit 5.
* Repeat these 2 rows 41 more times, still doing it as i-cord. When you do row 2 for the last time, change it slightly to knit 3, k2tog. You will have 4 stitches.
* Cut your yarn, leaving a 5-inch tail. Keep the "live" stitches on your needle, but anchor the loose tail by weaving it loosely through 1 or 2 stitches at the back of the i-cord strand just completed.
* Slide the live stitches from your needle onto a stitch holder. Cut your yarn, leaving a 5-inch tail to weave in later.

tip — "Live" stitches are stitches that are not bound off but that you are not working with at the moment. You often move them to a stitch holder while working on other stitches.

Make the second strand:

* Slide the next 4 stitches from the stitch holder onto your DPN.
* String 49 beads onto a new piece of working yarn.
* Attach the yarn securely by making a small slipknot about 4 inches from the yarn end. Put the slipknot of new yarn on the DPN to the right of your active stitches and knit it together with the first stitch. After this first stitch, knit 1, make 1, knit 2. You will have 5 stitches.
* Work rows 1 and 2 of the "slip bead" pattern 49 times. When you do row 2 for the last time, change it slightly to knit 2, k2tog. You will have 4 stitches.
* Cut the yarn and anchor the loose tail as you did for the first i-cord strand. Slide the live stitches from your needle onto the stitch holder.

Make the third strand:

* Make the third strand the same way. This time, string 53 beads onto a new piece of working yarn. Then repeat what you did for the second strand, above. This time, do *not* cut the yarn at the end.

Join the three strands:

* Slide all 12 stitches from the 3 i-cord strands in order onto your DPN. Stop knitting in i-cord and go back to using the needles as if they were straight needles, turning the work each time you start a new row.
* *Purl 2, p2tog* to end of row. You will have 9 stitches.
* Next row: Knit 1, *purl 1, knit 1* to end of row.
* Work in knit 1 purl 1 rib for 4 rows.
* Next row: Purl 1, knit 1, purl 1, k2tog, p2tog, knit 1, purl 1. You will have 7 stitches.
* Continue in knit 1, purl 1 rib for 5 rows.
* Next row: Purl 1, k2tog, p2tog, knit 1, purl 1. You will have 5 stitches.
* Next row: Knit 1, *purl 1, knit 1* to end of row.
* Next row: Purl 1, p2tog, p2tog. You will have 3 stitches.
* You'll now go back to knitting i-cord, so don't turn the work anymore.
* Next row: Knit, beginning i-cord.
* Knit 9 more rows, working in i-cord.
* Next row: K3tog (see "tip" on page 70). Cut yarn, leaving a 5-inch tail, and pull the tail through the last loop to bind off.

finishing

1. Attach a bead to one end of the necklace, tying it on with the yarn tail.

2. Make an i-cord long enough to fit around the bead, then form it into a loop by sewing the ends together. Attach the loop to the other end of the necklace.

3. Weave in all the ends. To weave in yarn ends that may be slippery, pass the ends through stitches on the back of the work at least three times, sewing into the yarn rather than around it to hold the ends firmly. Cut the yarn close to the work. To keep it from fraying, put a drop of Fray Check on the cut ends.

> **tip** K3tog (knit three stitches together) is exactly like k2tog, except you put your right-hand needle through the next three stitches on the left-hand needle instead of the next two stitches!

The necklace fastens with an 8mm glass bead on one end and an i-cord loop on the other.

using a stitch holder

Sometimes you need to move stitches to a stitch holder to "reserve" them while you do something else in the pattern. Moving stitches is easy.

> **tip** If you don't have a stitch holder, use a piece of scrap yarn instead. Just thread a tapestry needle with the extra yarn and slip it through the stitches, as in step 1. Then ditch the needle and loosely tie the loop of yarn together to hold the stitches in place.

1 Insert your stitch holder into the stitch on the needle that you want to move, as if you were purling.

2 Then pull it off the needle.

3 Continue with as many stitches as you want to reserve.

4 Then just "close" the stitch holder.

When you're ready to put the stitches back on your needle, open the stitch holder and carefully slide the stitches right back onto the needle.

Sparkly Wrist and Ankle Bracelets

PATTERN BY SIVIA HARDING

skills casting on, using double-pointed needles, knit stitch, increasing (make 1), decreasing (k2tog), using a stitch holder, binding off, weaving in ends, i-cord

These bracelets might just revolutionize your concept of jewelry. They are stretchy, comfortable, elegant, and wild—all at the same time. The bracelets have a very different look front and back, so you may want to make a few. It's fun to mix and match yarn and beads! One ball of yarn will make several bracelets. These directions are for 1-, 3-, and 6-strand bracelets.

finished measurements

5 inches around (Note: Measure around your wrist or ankle to find the length bracelet you want. i-cord strands are stretchy, but if you want a longer bracelet, add extra beads to each strand.)

tip This pattern has directions for 1-strand, 3-strand, and 6-strand options. Read through the pattern first to familiarize yourself with the directions. Simple changes for each bracelet (the number of stitches to knit) are in parentheses. Longer explanations are written out separately.

materials

* 1 skein of Lang Opal (or Opal Color) [58% nylon, 42% viscose; 155m per 50g ball] (Colors used here: 1-strand bracelet: red 61; 3-strand bracelet: variegated gold 98; 6-strand bracelet: variegated copper 15)
* 21 (63, 126) size 6/0 silver-lined crystal seed beads
* 1 (3, 6) 6mm bead(s) for the closure
* 2 size 4 (3.5mm) double-pointed needles (DPNs)
* Stitch holders

See page 67 for additional tools needed

gauge

Approximately 32 stitches/48 rows = 4 inches in garter stitch

10 rows = 1 inch in slip-bead i-cord

pattern

* String 21 beads onto the yarn with dental floss or a large-eyed beading needle. Push the beads down the yarn until you have 1 or 2 feet of unbeaded yarn free to work with.
* Cast on 5 (11, 20) stitches. You will be using the DPNs just like regular straight needles.
* Row 1: Knit.
* Row 2: Knit 2, *yarn over, k2tog, knit 1* to end of row.
* Knit 5 rows.
* Next row: Knit all stitches, then use make 1 method to add 0 (1, 4) stitches at end of row. You will have 5 (12, 24) stitches.
* Knit 5 (4, 4) stitches. If you're making the 3- or 6-strand bracelet, slide the remaining stitches on to a stitch holder.

Begin i-cord:

* You'll now start knitting i-cord (see page 90) with whatever stitches remain on your needle to make the first strand of the bracelet. Keep the needles in your same hands and do not turn the work. Push the stitches to the other end of the DPN. Bring the working yarn around the back of the work in preparation for knitting the next row.
* Next row:

  For 1-strand bracelet: Knit 5.

  For other bracelets: Knit 2, make 1, knit 2. You will have 5 stitches.

Begin "slip bead" pattern:

* Row 1: Knit 2, slip bead, knit 2.
* Row 2: Knit 5.
* Repeat these 2 rows 20 more times. If you're making the 3- or 6-strand bracelet, the last time you do row 2 change it slightly to knit 3, k2tog. You will have 5 (4, 4) stitches.
* Cut your yarn, leaving a 5-inch tail. Keep the "live" stitches on your needle, but anchor the loose tail by weaving it loosely through 1 or 2 stitches at the back of the i-cord just completed. If you're making the 1-strand bracelet, skip ahead to "Join the strands."

Make more strands (for 3- and 6-strand bracelets only):

* Slide the live stitches from the i-cord you just completed onto a stitch holder. Slide the first 4 stitches from your other stitch holder onto a DPN. This will be for your second strand.
* String 21 beads onto a new piece of working yarn.
* Attach the yarn securely by making a small slipknot about 4 inches from the yarn end. Put the slipknot of new yarn on the DPN to the right of your active stitches and knit it together with the first stitch.
* After this first stitch, knit 1, make 1, knit 2. You will have 5 stitches.
* Work rows 1 and 2 of the "slip bead" pattern 21 times.
* Cut the yarn and anchor the loose tail as you did for the first i-cord strand. Slide the live stitches from your needle onto a stitch holder.
* Make 1 (4) more i-cord(s) in the same manner using the remaining 4 (16) stitches, stringing 21 beads onto a new piece of working yarn before you begin each i-cord.
* Do not cut the yarn after knitting the last i-cord. Slide all 12 (24) stitches from the 3 (6) i-cord strands in order onto your DPN.

Join the strands:

* You'll now stop knitting i-cord and go back to using the DPNs as if they were straight needles, turning the work each time you start a new row.

* Next row:

    For 1-strand bracelet: Knit. You will have 5 stitches.

    For 3-strand bracelet: Knit 4, k2tog, knit 5. You will have 11 stiches.

    For 6-strand bracelet: *Knit 4, k2tog* to end of row. You will have 20 stitches.

* Knit 4 rows.

* Next row: Knit 2, *place bead (6mm bead), knit 2* to end of row.

* Knit 1 more row.

* Bind off all stitches.

finishing

Weave in the loose yarn end, then cut it close to the work and apply a drop of Fray Check to it.

web

Want to make a chocker to wear with the bracelets? Go to www.knitgrrl.com for directions.

The 1-strand bracelet

The 3-strand bracelet

The 6-strand bracelet. For this variation, the designer used three colors of yarn and three colors of beads to shake things up a bit. Use whatever color yarn and beads you want for a one-of-a-kind piece of jewelry!

bring it on

Just in case you're getting bored, here's a whole new twist. Circular needles and double-pointed needles allow you to knit tube shapes, setting you free to knit ponchos, bags, and lots more!

CIRCULAR NEEDLES

Working on circular needles is called **knitting in the round**. A poncho or hat knit in the round fits better and requires less shaping effort than one knit flat. When you work on circular needles, each row is called a **round**. Here's how to get started.

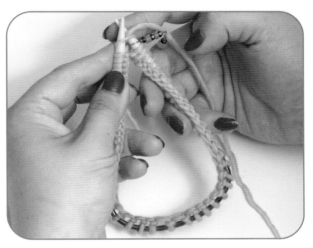

1 Cast on the required number of stitches, just as you would on straight needles. Then spread them out along the entire length of the needle. Line up the bottom loops of yarn so they're all running along the "bottom" of the needle. This will keep you from twisting the round when you start to knit. Don't skip this step, because you'll have to start again from the beginning if you do.

2 Place the needle tip that's connected to the yarn ball in your right (or dominant) hand and insert it into the first stitch on the left side. (Insert a stitch marker first if the pattern tells you to mark the beginning of the round, because that's where you are.) Now knit as usual.

3 When you get back to where you started, just keep going. The knit piece will form a tube. You may notice that the first stitch—the "connector" stitch—is a little loose for the first few rounds. It should tighten up if you tug gently on the loose yarn end.

tip Have stitch markers handy when you're knitting in the round—they will help you mark where you are in the pattern.

DOUBLE-POINTED NEEDLES

When you knit on double-pointed needles, or DPNs, each row is called a round, just as with circular needles. DPNs usually come in sets of four or five. To use them, you always leave one needle empty as your "working" needle. As you knit from a full needle onto the working needle, the full needle will empty and become your working needle.

When you first start using DPNs, you may find it awkward how the extra needles "dangle" when you're not using them. Don't worry, you'll get used to it! To keep the stitches from sliding off the dangling needles after casting on, just center the stitches in the middle of the needles.

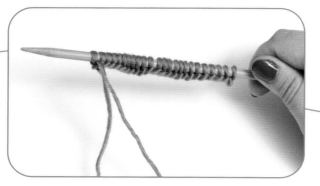

1 Cast all of the stitches needed onto one needle.

2 Divide the stitches evenly among three needles by slipping them from the first needle onto the other two. Until the round has been joined, the needles will hang loose in your hands, but that's okay.

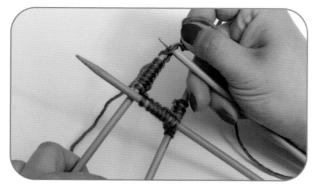

3 Hold the "working" (empty) needle in your dominant hand and knit from the start of the round. When you've knit all the stitches on the first DPN, it becomes your new working needle.

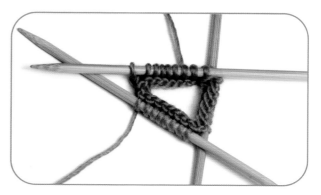

4 Knit all the way around. After knitting a few rounds, you'll see a small tube begin to take shape.

3-NEEDLE BIND OFF

3-needle bind off is a way to bind off and seam two knitted pieces at the same time. It makes a less bulky and neater seam. You need three needles of the same size.

1 If the stitches to be joined are on stitch holders, move them to separate needles. Place the knitted pieces' right (public) sides together.

2 Put a third needle through the first stitch on the front needle, and then through the first stitch on the back needle. Knit the two stitches together. Repeat with the second stitch on each needle.

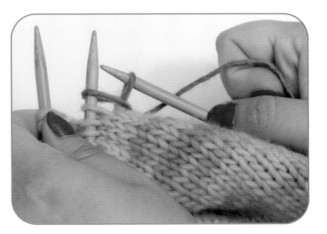

3 You now have two stitches on the third needle. Lift the stitch on the far right over the left stitch, binding off as usual.

4 Repeat steps 1–3 until all stitches are bound off and the two pieces are joined.

Sproingy Poncho

tip Denise needles come in handy with this pattern—it's easier to switch cords than needles as your poncho gets larger and larger.

PATTERN BY AMY R. SINGER

skills casting on, knitting in the round, using stitch markers, knit stitch, purl stitch, increasing (k1fb), joining new yarn, binding off, weaving in ends

This yarn is totally cool. It's made of stretchy synthetics—when you knit with it, the fabric sproings in every direction! Best of all, there's no need to worry about size. Too narrow? Just pull it! Too wide? Toss it in the wash (following the care instructions on the yarn label) and it goes back to its original size. All attempts to get a final measurement of the poncho were thwarted by it sproinging all over the place. However, many people of various sizes have tried on the poncho, and we haven't yet found anyone it doesn't fit! It really does contract and expand that much. The only trick with this yarn is that it needs quite a lot of ribbing to keep the edges from rolling. If you decide to knit it in a different yarn, you may want to use less ribbing—your call.

size
One size fits all

finished measurements
Chest: about 18 inches across
Length: about 20 inches

materials
* 15 balls of Crystal Palace Deco Ribbon [70% acrylic/ 30% nylon; 80 yds per 50g ball] (Color used here: Strawberry 9237)
* 1 24-inch size 10 (6mm) circular needle
* 1 24-inch size 11 (8mm) circular needle
* 1 36-inch or longer size 11 (8mm) circular needle
* 2 stitch markers in different colors
* Row counter
* Ruler
* Tapestry needle

gauge
Approximately 16 sts/22 rows = 4 inches in stockinette stitch

what's a stitch marker?

From the fanciest beaded marker to a plain piece of string or yarn tied in a loop, a stitch marker sits between two stitches on your needle to remind you to do something when you get to that particular stitch. In most patterns knit in the round, stitch markers help you keep track of where the round begins. In this pattern, they'll also remind you to increase in the next stitch. When you get to the marker, just slide it from your left-hand needle onto your right and keep going.

pattern
* Using the size 10 needle, cast on 100 stitches.
* Place the first color marker to indicate the beginning of the round, and join the work, being careful not to twist.
* Work in knit 2, purl 2 rib for 9 rounds. To do this: knit 2, bring the yarn forward between your needles, purl 2, put your yarn to the back again, knit 2 and repeat.
* Change to size 11 needle. Knit 50, place second color marker, knit 50.

Begin increasing:
* Round 1: Slip first color marker, k1fb, knit to 1 stitch before second color marker, k1fb, slip second color marker, k1fb, knit to 1 stitch before first color marker, k1fb.
* Round 2: Knit.
* Repeat these 2 rounds until poncho measures 16 inches from the top of the neck to the bottom of the point. When your work starts to get crowded on the needle, change to a longer one. (If you're using Denise needles, you can just switch to a longer cord.)
* Work in knit 2, purl 2 rib for 9 rounds.
* Bind off very loosely, using a larger size needle if necessary.

finishing
Weave in any loose ends.

Cropped Tank

PATTERN BY JENNA WILSON

skills casting on, knitting in the round, using stitch markers, knit stitch, purl stitch, decreasing (k2tog, p2tog, SSK), joining new yarn, picking up stitches, binding off, seaming, weaving in ends

This cute cropped tank top has side stripes and contrasting trim around the neck and armholes. The pattern has several parts, but if you work through it step by step you'll be fine. Itching for a shortcut? Just ignore the side panels, or, for a more deconstructed look, omit the finishing trim completely.

One thing about sizing: the dimensions of the top appear small in the schematic, but that's because the yarn we used, Cascade Fixation, stretches a *lot*. Use the chest measurements below to find your size—if you're unsure, go a size bigger. Also, the top is cropped quite short—if you're not into bare midriffs, simply increase the length of the front and back before you start decreasing for the armholes. (Remember that you'll need another skein or two of yarn, though!)

size
XS (S, M, L, XL)
Find your size by measuring around your chest:
XS: 27 inches around
S: 28½ inches
M: 30 inches
L: 32 inches
XL: 34 inches

measurements
These dimensions are for the *moderately* stretched front and back. The top stretches a lot when you put it on!

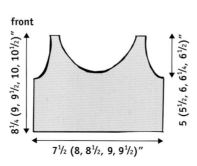

front

8¼ (9, 9½, 10, 10½)"

5 (5½, 6, 6¼, 6½)"

7½ (8, 8½, 9, 9½)"

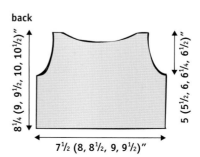

back

8¼ (9, 9½, 10, 10½)"

5 (5½, 6, 6¼, 6½)"

7½ (8, 8½, 9, 9½)"

materials

- [Color 1] 3 (3, 3, 4, 4) balls of Cascade Fixation [98.3% cotton, 1.7% elastic; 100 yds per 50g ball] (Color used here: 6399 lilac)
- [Color 2, for optional trim] 1 ball of Cascade Fixation [98.3% cotton, 1.7% elastic; 100 yds per 50g ball] (Color used here: 2137 light blue)
- 1 pair size 5 (3.75mm) straight needles (or size needed to match gauge when knitting back and forth)
- 1 24-inch size 5 (3.75mm) circular needle (or size needed to match gauge when knitting in the round)
- Stitch holders
- Row counter
- Ruler
- Tapestry needle

gauge

40 stitches and 38 rows = 4 inches in rib, unstretched
23 stitches and 39 rows = 4 inches in rib, moderately stretched

pattern

This pattern is knitted in two pieces: the back and the front, with two side panels that can be added by picking up stitches along the sides of the front piece. The back and front pieces and the side panels are knit flat (back and forth on straight needles). Everything is knitted in Color 1 unless otherwise stated. The neckline and armhole trim, knit in Color 2, is added later, picking up stitches and working on a circular needle.

> ## tip
> The term "work in pattern" means that you should knit or purl the stitches as they appear. If, on the side that's facing you, the stitch you are about to stick your needle into looks like a knit (a V-shape) then knit the stitch. If it looks like a purl (a bump), purl the stitch. Make sure to move the yarn from front to back *between* the needles, not over the top.

Back

- Using the straight needles, cast on 74 (78, 82, 90, 94) stitches.
- Row 1 (right side): *Knit 2, purl 2 * to last 2 stitches, then knit 2.
- Row 2 (wrong side): *Purl 2, knit 2* to last 2 stitches, then purl 2.
- Repeat rows 1 and 2 for 8¼ (9, 9½, 10, 10½) inches, ending with row 2. If you'd like the tank top to be longer, keep repeating rows 1 and 2 until you are satisfied with the length. Just be sure you end with row 2.

Shape the armhole:

- Row 1 (right side): Knit 1, SSK, then work in pattern to last 3 stitches, k2tog, knit 1.
- Row 2 (wrong side): Work in pattern for the whole row.
- Repeat these 2 rows 3 (3, 5, 7, 7) more times. You will have 66 (70, 70, 74, 78) stitches.
- Work in pattern without increasing or decreasing, until the piece measures 3¼ (3¼, 3¼, 3¾, 3¾) inches from beginning of armhole shaping.

Shape the neck:

- Work 20 (20, 20, 20, 22) stitches in pattern, bind off 26 (30, 30, 34, 34) stitches, then work remaining 20 (20, 20, 20, 22) stitches in pattern. You should have 2 sections of 20 stitches each on your needle, with a big gap in the middle. Yarn is at left side.

Shape first side of neck and strap:

- Row 1 (wrong side): Work in pattern to last 2 stitches, then k2tog.
- Row 2 (right side): Bind off 3 stitches, then work in pattern to end of row.
- Row 3: Work in pattern to last 2 stitches, k2tog.
- Row 4: Bind off 1 stitch, then work in pattern to end of row.
- Rows 5, 7, 9, 11: Work in pattern to end of row.
- Rows 6, 8, 10, 12: SSK, then work in pattern to end of row. When you finish row 12, you will have 10 (10, 10, 10, 12) stitches.
- After row 12, work 6 (10, 14, 14, 16) more rows in pattern without increasing or decreasing. If you want a longer shoulder strap, knit extra rows at this point until it's the length you want.
- Slip these strap stitches onto a stitch holder and cut the yarn, leaving a 6-inch tail.

Shape second side of neck and strap:

* With the right side facing you, join new yarn at the right side of back.
* Row 1 (right side): Work in pattern to last 2 stitches, then p2tog.
* Row 2 (wrong side): Bind off 3 stitches, work in pattern to end of row.
* Row 3: Work in pattern to last 2 stitches, then p2tog.
* Row 4: Bind off 1 stitch, then work in pattern to end of row.
* Rows 5, 7, 9, 11, 13: Work in pattern to end of row.
* Rows 6, 8, 10, 12: P2tog, then work in pattern to end of row. When you finish row 12, you will have 10 (10, 10, 10, 12) stitches.
* After row 12, work 6 (10, 14, 14, 16) more rows in pattern without increasing or decreasing. If you made the first strap longer, knit extra rows at this point until this strap is the same length.
* Slip these strap stitches onto a stitch holder and cut the yarn, leaving a 6-inch tail.

Front

* Repeat the instructions for the back up to "Shape the armhole." Then proceed as follows.
* Next row (right side): Knit 1, SSK, then work in pattern to last 3 stitches, k2tog, knit 1.
* Next row (wrong side): Work first 29 (29, 31, 33, 35) stitches in pattern, bind off 14 (18, 18, 22, 22) stitches, then work remaining 29 (29, 31, 33, 35) stitches in pattern.

Shape first side of neck and strap:

* Rows 1, 3, and 5 (right side): Knit 1, SSK, work in pattern to last 2 stitches, k2tog.
* Row 2 (wrong side): Bind off 3 stitches, then work in pattern to end of row.
* Rows 4 and 6: P2tog, then work in pattern to end of row.
* Row 7: For sizes XS and S, work in pattern to last 2 stitches, then k2tog. For all other sizes, repeat row 1.
* Row 8 and all even-numbered rows to row 30: Work even in pattern.
* Row 9: For sizes XS and S, work in pattern to last 2 stitches, then k2tog. For all other sizes, repeat row 1.

* Rows 11 and 13: For sizes XS, S, and M, work in pattern to last 2 stitches, then k2tog. For all other sizes, repeat row 1.
* Rows 15, 19, 23, and 27: Work in pattern.
* Rows 17, 21, 25, and 29: Work in pattern to last 2 stitches, then k2tog.
* When you finish row 30, you will have 10 (10, 10, 10, 12) stitches.
* Once 30 rows are complete, work in pattern without increasing or decreasing for 18 (22, 28, 30, 32) more rows, or until the front measures the same as the back from hem to top of shoulder strap. Slip left strap stitches onto a stitch holder and cut the yarn, leaving a 6-inch tail.

Shape second side of neck and strap:

* With the right side facing you, join new yarn at neck edge.
* Row 1 (right side): Bind off 3 stitches, work in pattern to last 3 stitches, k2tog, knit 1.
* Rows 2, 4, and 6 (wrong side): Work in pattern to last 2 stitches, p2tog.
* Rows 3 and 5: SSK, work in pattern to last 3 stitches, k2tog, knit 1.
* Row 7: For sizes XS and S, SSK, then work in pattern to end of row. For all other sizes, repeat row 3.
* Rows 8 and all even-numbered rows to row 30: Work even in pattern.
* Row 9: For sizes XS and S, SSK, then work in pattern to end of row. For all other sizes, repeat row 3.
* Rows 11 and 13: For sizes XS, S, and M, SSK, then work in pattern to end of row. For all other sizes, repeat row 3.
* Rows 15, 19, 23, and 27: Work in pattern without increasing or decreasing.
* Rows 17, 21, 25, and 29: SSK, then work in pattern to end of row.
* When you finish row 30, you will have 10 (10, 10, 10, 12) stitches.
* Once 30 rows are complete, work in pattern without increasing or decreasing for 18 (22, 28, 30, 32) more rows, or until this side matches the left side. Slip right strap stitches onto a stitch holder and cut the yarn, leaving a 6-inch tail.

Side panels

* Using Color 2, pick up 52 (56, 60, 64, 66) stitches evenly along the left side edge of the front, between the hem and armhole. (If you adjusted the length of the body, you will need to adjust the number of stitches picked up. You should pick up 2 stitches for every 3 rows of knitting.)
* With the right side facing you, purl 1 row.
* Knit 1 row.
* Switch to Color 1 (see "Joining new yarn," on page 26), but do not cut Color 2. Work in stockinette (knit 1 row, purl 1 row) for 6 rows using Color 1.
* The right side should be facing you. Switch back to Color 2, then knit 2 rows.
* Purl 1 row.
* Bind off.
* Repeat for the right side panel, picking up stitches along the right side of the front piece.

Here's what the side panel will look like.

finishing

1. Seam the side panels to the back.

2. Use the 3-needle bind-off method (see page 77) and size 5 straight needles to join the straps from the front and back pieces at the shoulders. If you want, you can also just bind off each edge normally and then seam them together.

Neck and armhole trim

Trim around neck:

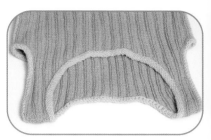

Optional trim is added around the neck and armholes.

* Using Color 2 and the circular needle, start at one shoulder and pick up 72 (80, 88, 94, 98) stitches along the front neck edge and 44 (52, 56, 60, 62) stitches along the back neck edge. (Try to space your picked-up stitches evenly around the neck. It's a good idea to count the number of stitches you need to pick up and "plan" it out first, making sure you do an equal number on each side of the neck.)
* Join to knit in the round, placing a stitch marker at the beginning of the round.
* With the right side facing you, purl 4 rounds.
* Cut the yarn, leaving a tail long enough to sew all around the neckline.
* Fold the new trim over so the raw edge is inside and sew it down using a tapestry needle and the long yarn tail. The raw edge of the neckline should now be hidden underneath the trim.

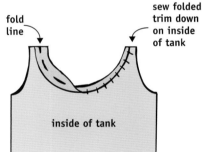

fold line

sew folded trim down on inside of tank

inside of tank

Trim around armholes:

* Using Color 2 and the circular needle, pick up 61 (65, 73, 77, 77) stitches around one armhole. Make sure your picked-up stitches are spaced evenly around the armhole, with the same number on each side.
* Join to knit in the round, placing a stitch marker at the beginning of the round.
* With the right side facing you, purl 3 rounds.
* Cut the yarn, leaving a tail long enough to sew all around the armhole.
* Fold the new trim over so the raw edge is inside and sew it down as you did for the neckline, hiding the raw edge.
* Repeat for the other armhole.
* Weave in any loose ends.

Cabana Beach Bag

PATTERN BY LUCY H. LEE

skills casting on, knitting in the round, using stitch markers, knit stitch, purl stitch, increasing (k1fb, make 1, cable cast-on), decreasing (k2tog, k2tog tbl), yarn over, joining new yarn, binding off, weaving in ends, seaming, i-cord, using double-pointed needles (for the i-cord), blocking (optional)

Lucy's inspiration for this bag came from the little striped tents, called *cabanas*, that people used for changing into their bathing suits on the beach in the early 1900s. If you prefer, you can knit the bag in a solid color, using 5 skeins of one color. The bag is knit solidly—no holes for your beach gear to fall through. The straps of the beach bag are sewn to the body so it can be worn as a backpack. A cell phone/ sunglass case and a key ring are attached with separate i-cords.

finished measurements

The main bag is 15 inches tall x 28 inches around.

materials

* [Color 1] 3 skeins of Cascade Sierra Quatro yarn [80% pima cotton, 20% wool; 191 yds per 100g skein] (Color used here: 81)
* [Color 2] 2 skeins of Cascade Sierra Quatro yarn [80% pima cotton, 20% wool; 191 yds per 100g skein] (Color used here: 90)
* 1 26-inch size 8 (5mm) circular needle
* 1 16-inch size 3 (3.25mm) circular needle
* 1 26-inch size 3 (3.25mm) circular needle
* 1 pair size 3 (3.25mm) straight needles
* 5 size 3 (3.25mm) double-pointed needles (DPNs)
* Stitch markers—you'll need at least 16, one of them a different color
* Row counter
* Tapestry needle
* Sewing needle and thread to match yarn
* 1 ¾-inch button
* 1 shank clip or key ring
* 1 large safety pin

gauge

25 stitches/20 rows = 4 inches on size 8 needles in vertical stripe pattern. (Note: Gauge is not critical, as long as the knit fabric is firm.)

pattern/main bag

The vertical stripe pattern of this bag is made by alternating 1 stitch of Color 1 with 1 stitch of Color 2. The best and quickest way to do this is to hold one color in each hand and knit "two-handed." I recommend carrying Color 1 in your left hand (or nondominant hand) and Color 2 in your right (or dominant) hand. Try it both ways in your swatch to see which you like better. If you just can't get the swing of the two-handed thing, you can hold both strands in one hand, as usual, and just switch back and forth between them.

Start at bottom of main bag:

* With Color 1 and size 3 DPNs, cast on 8 stitches and divide among 4 needles, forming a circle. Place stitch marker (the contrasting color one) to mark beginning of round.
* Round 1: K1fb in every stitch. You will have 16 stitches.
* Round 2: Purl.
* Round 3: Repeat round 1. You will have 32 stitches.
* Round 4: Purl.
* Round 5: *Knit 2, slide on a new marker* to end of round. You will have placed 16 markers.
* Round 6: Purl.
* Round 7: *Slip marker, k1fb, knit to next marker* to end of round. You will have 48 stitches.
* Round 8: Purl.
* Round 9: Knit.
* Round 10: Purl.
* Repeat rounds 7–10 until there are 192 stitches. When your knitting gets too squished, change to the 16-inch circular needle.

Now start body of bag:

* Change to 26-inch size 8 circular needle and begin the Vertical Stripe Pattern, as follows. You can remove all the markers except the one at the beginning of the round.
* Next row (Vertical Stripe Pattern): *Knit 1 with Color 1, knit 1 with Color 2* to end of round.

changing needles

To change from DPNs to a circular needle, or from a smaller circular needle to a larger one, start at the beginning of the round and slip the stitches, one by one, from one needle to the other, as if you were transferring the stitches to a stitch holder. If you prefer, you can simply start knitting onto the circular needle at the beginning of a round and put aside the double-pointed needles (or the smaller circular needle) as you work your way around.

* Work in pattern, following the Vertical Stripe pattern, until the bag measures 13 inches from where you began the stripes.
* Change to 26-inch size 3 circular needle and use Color 1 only to decrease as follows: *Knit 6, k2tog * to end of round. You will have 168 stitches.
* Change to size 3 straight needles.

Start top of bag:

The top of the bag is knit in garter stitch (knit every row) on straight needles. Later, it will be folded over to form a sleeve for the drawstring.

* Next row: Slip the first stitch purlwise with yarn in front. To do this, move the yarn between the needles so it's in front and insert your needle into the stitch as if you were about to purl, sliding the stitch to the right-hand needle. Knit rest of row.
* Repeat this row for 2½ inches, then bind off.

Drawstring strap

This is a long piece of i-cord with a knitted "tab" at each end, that will form the backpack straps.

Make the first tab:

* Using the size 3 DPNs and Color 2, cast on 3 stitches. You are going to start by using the DPNs as if they were straight needles, turning the work after each row.
* Row 1: Knit.
* Row 2: Knit 1, make 1, knit 1, make 1, knit 1. You will have 5 stitches.

* Row 3: Knit.
* Row 4: Knit 1, make 1, knit 3, make 1, knit 1. You will have 7 stitches.
* Row 5: Knit.
* Row 6: Knit 1, make 1, knit 5, make 1, knit 1. You will have 9 stitches.
* Rows 7–15: Knit.
* Row 16: Knit 1, k2tog, knit 3, k2tog, knit 1. You will have 7 stitches.
* Row 17: Knit.
* Row 18: Knit 1, k2tog, knit 1, k2tog, knit 1. You will have 5 stitches.
* Row 19: Knit.

Begin i-cord:

* You are now going to make a long i-cord with the remaining 5 stitches (see page 90). Remember not to turn the work after each row.

Make the second tab:

* Now you'll stop making i-cord and go back to using the DPNs like straight needles, turning your knitting after each row.
* Row 1: Knit 1, make 1, knit 3, make 1, knit 1. You will have 7 stitches.
* Row 2: Knit.
* Row 3: Knit 1, make 1, knit 5, make 1, knit 1. You will have 9 stitches.
* Rows 4–12: Knit.
* Row 13: Knit 1, knit 1, k2tog, knit 3, k2tog, knit 1. You will have 7 stitches.
* Row 14: Knit.
* Row 15: Knit 1, k2tog, knit 1, k2tog, knit 1. You will have 5 stitches.
* Row 16: Knit.
* Row 17: Knit 1, k3tog, knit 1. You will have 3 stitches. (Note: K3tog is the same as k2tog except you put your needle through 3 stitches instead of 2.)
* Row 18: Knit.
* Row 19: K3tog. You will have 1 stitch.
* Cut the yarn, leaving a tail. Slip the tail through the remaining loop and pull to secure.

finishing

1. Sew up the hole in the bottom of the bag (where you started knitting).

2. To create a sleeve for the drawstring, fold the flap at the top of the bag in half and sew it all around to the inside of the bag.

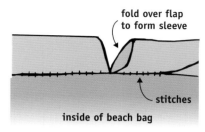

fold over flap to form sleeve

stitches

inside of beach bag

3. To attach the drawstring, attach a safety pin to one of the tabs and pull it all the way through the sleeve. The drawstring will double as backpack straps—sew down each tab to the side of the bag about 4 inches on either side of the center.

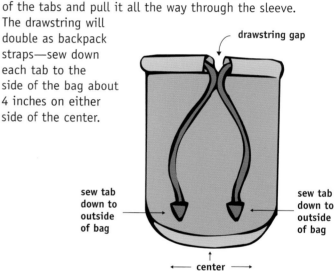

drawstring gap

sew tab down to outside of bag

sew tab down to outside of bag

center

4" 4"

4. Weave in any loose ends. You can lightly block the bottom of the bag if you like (see page 47).

pattern / cell phone case

The cell phone case is knit in one piece, then folded and sewn together.

* Using size 3 straight needles and Color 2, cast on 22 stitches.
* Knit all rows until piece measures 6½ inches.
* Next 2 rows: Bind off 3 stitches, knit to end of row. You will have 16 stitches.
* Knit 10 rows.
* Next 2 rows: Cast on 3 stitches with cable cast-on, then knit to end of row. You will have 22 stitches.
* Knit all rows until piece measures 14 inches.
* Next row: Knit 10, k2tog, knit 10. You will have 21 stitches.
* Next row: Slip 1 stitch purlwise with yarn held in front, then bring the yarn to the back (between the needles) and knit to end of row.
* Repeat this row 5 more times.

Begin decreasing:

* Row 1: Slip 1 purlwise with yarn in front, k2tog tbl, knit to last 3 stitches, k2tog, knit 1.
* Row 2: Knit.
* Repeat rows 1 and 2 until you have only 11 stitches.

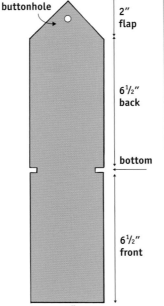

buttonhole

2" flap

6½" back

bottom

6½" front

4"

Make the buttonhole:

* Row 1: Slip 1 stitch purlwise, k2tog tbl, knit 2, yarn over, k2tog, knit 1, k2tog, knit 1.
* Row 2: Knit.
* Repeat rows 1 and 2 until you have only 5 stitches.
* Next row: Knit 1, k3tog, knit 1.
* Next row: Knit.
* Next row: K3tog. Cut the yarn, leaving a tail. Slip the tail through the remaining loop and pull to secure.

Cords for cell phone case and key clip (make 2)

* Using 2 size 3 DPNs and Color 2, cast on 4 stitches.
* Make a 16-inch long i-cord (see page 90).
* Bind off.

finishing

1. Weave in any loose ends.

2. Lay the case flat, right side up. Fold up the bottom to form the case and sew the side seams. Turn the case right side out.

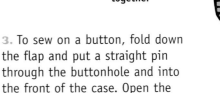

sew sides together

fold up bottom half

3. To sew on a button, fold down the flap and put a straight pin through the buttonhole and into the front of the case. Open the flap and sew a button at the pin mark.

4. Sew the two 16-inch i-cords to the inside of the bag, one on either side of the drawstring gap.

5. Sew the end of one i-cord to the top corner of the cell phone case. Sew the other i-cord to your shank clip/key ring.

Got your cell phone and your keys and you're set to go! I-cords attach the cell phone case and the key ring to the inside of the beach bag so you'll always know where they are.

extra toppings

Treat your knitting projects to something extra! Add these fun embellishments to any knitted hat, scarf, or bag to take it from so-so to something special. It's just like extra foam on your mochaccino—why *wouldn't* you want it?

TASSELS

Tassels are great for decorating the ends of a scarf or a belt. They're easy to make, too. Here's how.

1 Cut lengths of yarn that are twice as long as you want the tassel to be. The more pieces of yarn you have, the thicker the tassel will be.

2 Tie a separate length of yarn around the center of the bundle of yarn to secure all the pieces and knot the tie. Trim the ends of the tie equal with the yarn pieces.

3 Fold the bundle of yarn ends in half and wrap a separate piece of yarn around the tassel near the top to secure it.

BRAIDS

You probably already know how to braid—but just in case, here's a refresher. Try braiding the fringe on a scarf or belt for a unique look.

To make a braid, tie three strands of yarn together at one end. bring the left strand over the center strand. Then bring the right strand over the center strand. Repeat these two steps. At the end, make a knot with all three strands.

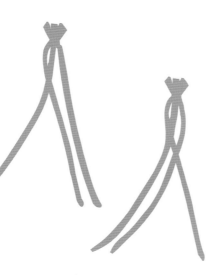

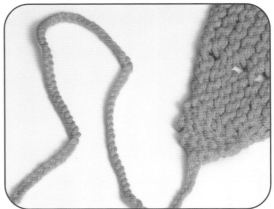

A braid makes a sturdy tie on a headband, belt, or kerchief.

I-CORD

I-cord is great for trimming the edges of hats, scarves, beach bags, and just about anything else. It's also fun to bend into shapes or wind all over a hat or scarf and then sew down with the same yarn threaded through a tapestry needle. Here's how to make it.

pattern

* Cast on 3–5 stitches, depending on how thick you want the cord, onto a double-pointed needle (DPN).
* Knit the first row (using a second DPN).
* Keep the same needle in your left (or nondominant) hand, but slide the knitting to the other side of the needle.
* Pull the thread tight across the back of the stitches and knit the next row.

To knit i-cord, slide the stitches to the other side of the needle and pull the yarn tight across the back as you knit the next row.

* Slide the knitting across again, and knit another row.
* After knitting back and forth a few rows, tug on the bottom of the knitted tube that is developing. You'll see it even out and turn into a nice, smooth cord.

i-cord flowers

Use i-cord to make flowers to decorate a headband (such as the Blossom Headband on page 46) or to add to a sweater or purse. Here's how to do it.

1. For each flower, make an i-cord 18 inches long.

2. Lay the cord out flat and mark off every 3 inches with a straight pin.

straight pins

3"

3. To make the first loop, or petal, bring the beginning end of the i-cord to the first pin. Remove the pin. With sewing needle and thread, sew the end to the i-cord.

sew here

4. Make a loop with the next 3-inch piece of i-cord and sew the base of this loop to the first loop.

5. Continue this way until you have made all 6 petals. With sewing needle and thread, sew the flower to the headband. Sew a bead or a button in the center of each flower.

6. Repeat for as many flowers as you want.

Color Your World

What if you know *exactly* the color you want, but can't find it in the store? No problem—just make it yourself! Believe it or not, you can use powdered Kool-Aid to dye yarn a whole bunch of colors.

THE DYE Each ounce of yarn needs at least one packet of drink mix, so if you have an 8-ounce skein, you'll need at least eight packets. The more Kool-Aid you use, the darker the color will be. For a custom color, try mixing two different flavors of Kool-Aid—strawberry and black cherry, for example—to make your own shade of red.

THE YARN This dyeing technique only works on wool and animal fibers such as alpaca and mohair. Cotton and synthetics (nylon, acrylic) will not dye. If your yarn is a mix of two or more fiber types, try dyeing a swatch first. White yarn will give you the truest color but you could also dye over light-colored yarn.

THE CONTAINER Use one large enough to fit all of the yarn. A glass or Pyrex container is best because it won't absorb the colors like a plastic one will. Or use a microwave-safe deli container you can throw away afterward.

THE PROCEDURE

* Wind the yarn into a loose circle or skein. Don't try to dye a ball of yarn because dye won't get into the center. Put the yarn into the sink or a bowl of room-temperature water and soak it well.

* Put on the gloves. Empty the drink-mix packets into the microwave-safe container and add a little water. Stir until dissolved.

* Carefully lift the yarn out of the water and *gently* squeeze out some of the excess water. Put the wet yarn into the dye, adding enough water to cover the yarn.

* Cover the container. Microwave on high power for 5 minutes. Check to see if the yarn has absorbed all the color (the water will be mostly clear). If not, wait a few minutes and then microwave again for 2 more minutes. Check again. Still not clear? Give it 2 more minutes.

* Do not rinse the yarn yet! Let it cool until it is again at room temperature. Otherwise, you risk felting it (shrinking the fibers).

* Using room-temperature water, rinse the yarn, gently squeezing it, and hang it to dry either over the faucet in your bathtub or outside in your backyard. Once it's dry, you can start knitting with it!

* The yarn is now colorfast, but to be safe you may want to wash your knitted items in cold water.

YOU WILL NEED:

* A microwave-safe dish with lid
* Yarn
* Packets of powdered Kool-Aid drink mix
* Spoon
* Dishwashing gloves (optional, but good to have)

logging out...

Need help? Want inspiration? Knitting is all about friends and community—odds are, you'll never be far from someone who's happy to help you! Here are some last-minute tips for making your knitting life a happy one.

CARE INSTRUCTIONS

Hand-knit items should be washed in cold or slightly warm water with a very mild soap—or even cheap shampoo! If you are washing knits in the sink, do not run water directly onto them (this can cause slight felting). Here's how to hand wash knits the right way:

1. Fill the sink or container you're using with cold or room-temperature water. Add soap or shampoo (not too much!) and swish it around.

2. Add the knitted item and push it under the water. Don't swish it around; just let it soak for a while, weighted down with a dinner plate if it floats to the surface. If the water is very soapy after soaking, take out the item and change the water. Don't run fresh water directly onto your knits—you might accidentally felt them a little if the water temperatures are different.

3. Lay out a clean towel on the floor (or on a big table you don't mind getting wet). Lift up the item with both hands, supporting its weight from the bottom (wet wool is stretchy and can easily be pulled out of shape), and place it on the towel.

4. Roll up the towel and step on it a few times to remove as much water from your knit as possible. (You may need more towels, depending on the size of the item).

5. Place the now slightly damp item flat on another dry towel (or drying rack) and allow to air dry.

These directions can also be used to wash any kind of wool items. And if you follow them, you'll never have to worry about shrinking something that you took many hours to make. How great is that!

tip Always handle wet knitted items carefully, picking them up with both hands from the bottom so you don't stretch them out of shape.

web

Visit
www.knitgrrl.com
for help!

knitgrrl.com

PLACES to GO, THINGS to READ

Here's a list of some of my favorite yarn companies, crafty websites, magazines, places to buy yarn and supplies online, and organizations to look into.

YARN COMPANIES FEATURED IN knitgrrl 2

Brown Sheep: http://www.brownsheep.com

Cascade Yarns: http://www.cascadeyarns.com

Crystal Palace: http://www.straw.com/cpy

Lana Grossa: http://www.lanagrossa.com

Lang Yarns: http://www.langyarns.ch/en

Lion Brand: http://www.lionbrand.com

Rowan Yarn: http://www.knitrowan.com

ONLINE KNITTING AND CRAFTY RESOURCES

Knitgrrl: http://www.knitgrrl.com

Knitty: http://www.knitty.com

Knitter's Review: http://www.knittersreview.com

Woolworks: http://www.woolworks.org

Craftster: http://www.craftster.org

Glitter: http://www.supernaturale.com/glitter

Knitting for charity:
http://www.woolworks.org/charity.html

MAGAZINES

knit.1: http://www.knit1mag.com

Knitter's: http://www.knitters.com

Interweave Knits: http://www.interweave.com/knits

Vogue Knitting: http://www.vogueknitting.com

ONLINE YARN AND SUPPLIES

Denise Needles: http://www.knitdenise.com

Paper Source: http://www.paper-source.com

Threadbear Fiber Arts:
http://www.threadbearfiberarts.com

ORGANIZATIONS

Craft Yarn Council of America:
http://www.yarnstandards.com

The Knitter's Guild of America (TKGA):
http://www.tkga.org

MEET the DESIGNERS

T a-da! Here are the talented women who created the projects in this book. Want to meet them? Just come to knitgrrl.com and drop them a line.

JENNA ADORNO (Blossom Headband/Chocker) lives in Seattle with her partner and child. She has appeared on *Knitty Gritty*, in *Knitty.com* and many other publications. Her passion is designing hip, stylish garments that really fit.

KERRIE ALLMAN (Workout Water Bottle Holder) lives in London, England, where she runs an online knitting magazine called *MagKnits.com* filled with fun patterns.

SIVIA HARDING (Vintage Necklace, Sparkly Wrist and Ankle Bracelets) designs knitwear and knitted jewelry in Vancouver, Canada.

STEFANIE JAPEL (Beach-Read Book Covers) is an American high-pressure geochemist. She knits, lives, and works in Mainz, Germany. She designs almost everything she knits.

LUCY H. LEE (Cabana Beach Bag) owns Mind's Eye Yarns in Cambridge, Massachusetts, where she spins, dyes, knits, and does just about everything imaginable with yarn.

KIMBERLI MACKAY (Striped Pencil Purse, Beauty-to-Go Bag) works in New York City and knits as much as she possibly can, usually on long, work-related plane trips!

KRISTI PORTER (Striped Cardigan) did all the technical editing for this book (in other words, she made sure all the patterns worked!) from her home in sunny California. She works for *Knitty.com* and writes knitting books.

MEGAN REARDON (Boho Belt, Glo-Girl Kerchief) lives in Seattle, where she crafts constantly.

AMY SINGER (Sproingy Poncho) founded *Knitty.com*, an online knitting magazine that recently welcomed its five-millionth visitor! She's also somehow found the time to write three books on knitting.

JENNA WILSON (Cropped Tank) lives, knits, works, and eats in Toronto, Canada, which is fortunately a pretty good place to live in terms of yarn shops, employment, and restaurants. After studying physics, Jenna decided to take up knitting and law, and now she's an intellectual property lawyer who designs knitting patterns on the side.

KIRSTEN ZERBINIS (Full-of-Holes Scarf) lives in Ontario, Canada, where she designs beautiful knitwear.

SHANNON OKEY (Ooh-La-La Flip-Flops, Furry Denim Jacket Collar) lives in Cleveland, Ohio, with her partner Tamas, her dachshund, Anezka, and their naughty young cat, Spike. When she's not knitting or writing, she runs an online store filled with crafty goodness called **anezka handmade** and keeps the knitgrrl.com site running. She's currently writing two new books: one on spinning your own yarn, and one with Knitgrrl designer Heather Brack on felting. Spike still likes to steal yarn, which makes knitting anything take longer!

INDEX